"Tiger Woods Made Me Look Like a Genius"

DON CROSBY WITH JAMES DALE

"Tiger Woods Made Me Look Like a Genius"

Five Simple Ways to Take Ten Strokes Off Your Game

**Andrews McMeel
Publishing**

Kansas City

00 01 02 03 04 QUF 10 9 8 7 6 5 4 3 2 1

Library of Congress Cataloging-in-Publication Data
Crosby, Don, 1941-
    Tiger Woods mad me look like a genius : 5 simple ways to take 10 strokes off your
game / Don Crosby with James Dale.
        p. cm.
    ISBN 0-7407-0472-9 (pbk.)
        1. Golf—Study and teaching. I. Title: 5 simple ways to take 10 strokes off your game.
    II. Dale, Jim, 1948- III. Title.
GV962.5 .C76 2000
796.352'3—dc21
                                                                              99-042117

Design and composition by Lee Fukui

To the memory of Dad and Mom, David L. Crosby (1913–1998) and Bessie A. Crosby (1917–1999). To my wife, Faith, of thirty-six years—thanks for your support and love. Without you, none of this would have been possible.

To our children, David, Mike, and April—after thirty-four years of coaching, my favorite recollections are of our sons and daughter in sports. Thanks for the memories.

—Don Crosby

To the golfers in my life: Evelyn, Mark, Bob, Julie, Edwina, Bobby, Danny, Cathy, Phyllis, Stan, Joyce, and, of course, Don. Three club champs, four hustlers, two picture-perfect swings, several long-ball hitters, and one superb teacher. You'd think with all this talent around me, I'd be better at the game. Thank goodness I can write about it.

To my favorite threesome, Andy, Sara, and Alex.

To Ellen, the best partner there is.

—Jim Dale

CONTENTS

I'm a golf coach,
Not a golf pro.
I don't get paid by the lesson.
If I win, I get to keep my job.

Hi, my name is Don Crosby, and my job is to help you play as well as you can, as quickly as possible. That means making the most of the talent you've got. I'm not here to change your swing or teach you a weird grip or tell you to go out and buy a new set of expensive clubs. I'm here to lower your score to win matches. And one more thing: to make sure you have fun. If the game isn't fun—if it's a pain—you might as well play football without pads.

That's pretty much what I tell my Western High golf teams each year; it's what I told them in 1991, the year a kid named Tiger Woods joined the team as a freshman. Now this isn't just my personal philosophy. It's a matter of practicality. Our season is only twelve weeks long, so we have to make the team as good as it can be, fast. We don't have the luxury of tinkering with the arc of a kid's backswing for a month. We have six matches to play in that time.

So, each season we work on Crosby's Five, five basics that can lower your score, practically, simply, and quickly. Depending on what my player is shooting to begin with, each of Crosby's Five can save one to three shots per round, or an average of ten strokes if the player practices them diligently.

It so happens, my approach meshed perfectly with Tiger's. Nobody believes in the basics more than he does. Everything I preached reinforced what he practiced, which set a great example for his teammates, who started doing what he did. (Needless to say, we weren't expecting to take ten shots off Tiger's game. One or two would be more than enough.)

I've been a teacher and a coach of one sport or another for over thirty years. I've coached literally thousands of athletes—athletes with talent, with heart, with good attitudes and not-so-good. Teams that won championships and teams that blew them. And I've coached a few real stars. The first was running back Terry Metcalf at Long Beach State, where I was a defensive line coach at the time. Then David Wilson when he was a quarterback at Katella High School. (David went on to be a starter for the New Orleans Saints.) Next there was Todd Marinovich, who I coached in youth football in the late seventies. Even at that early stage, you knew you were looking at a future star. And most recently, there was Tiger, from '91 to '94.

After Tiger graduated I was looking back at what I do and I started thinking. Maybe what a lot of weekend golfers need more than a pro is a coach, somebody who can make the most of what they have as soon as possible. See, I've never been paid by the lesson, so I don't get to fiddle with your hook or your slice for five or six lessons at $75 a crack where, frankly, the slower we get it fixed the more money I make. No, I get measured real simply. Did my team win? If they did, I get to keep my job. If they didn't, I get another season or two to make sure they start winning. If they still don't, I might find myself being assistant manager for JV field hockey. Try and find a country club pro who ever lost his or her job because the members weren't playing well enough.

So, I decided to write down what I've been doing all these years. I wrote the techniques I teach (Crosby's Five), and I wrote the stories I've lived (Crosby's True Tales). I discovered there's a connection between them: They're both lessons that help you play better. The techniques give you the mechanics. The stories bring them to life—you can see how they worked for somebody else and how they may work for you. Put the techniques and the stories together and you get results. (I believe in results. If you do all the things an expert tells you to do and you still don't get results, I say you should get your money back.)

One more thing. Like everything I do, I try to make golf simple and fun. I don't like things that are harder than they have to be, and I hate things that aren't fun when they're supposed to be.

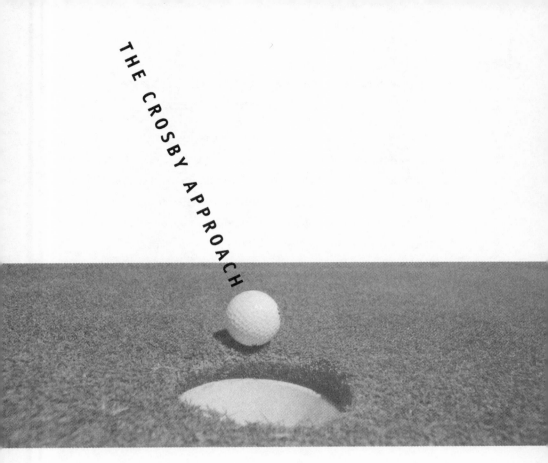

**Crosby's Five—basics
that can take ten strokes
off your game.**

INSIGHT:
Work on Things You Can Change.
Leave the Rest Alone.

Do you want to become a better golfer, or do you want to become a professional golfer on the PGA Tour? I can help you with the first, not the second. I make players better fast. I do it by working only on the parts of the game that can affect your score the most. I don't so much make every shot perfect; I just get you to hit fewer shots. That's my idea of practice.

A few words about
PRACTICE,
the most misunderstood aspect of the game of golf.

1. **Don't just practice.** Repeating mistakes doesn't make them go away; it turns them into bad habits. If you have a recurrent nasty slice, go out to the practice tee once a week, hit a hundred balls, and you'll learn to slice every time.

2. **Practice smart.** The fastest, most effective way to lower your score permanently is with smart practice. Not just practice, but smart practice. Learn the limits of each club. Gain the benefits of consistency. Use roll and bite. Play the angles of the course. Hit the shot that has the best chance to succeed.

3. **If you don't like practice, you're doing it wrong.** Practice shouldn't be boring or repetitious. It should be fun. Create games. Name exercises. Imagine fairways, rough, and water hazards when you're on the practice tee. Count how many chip shots hit the pin. Bet with your friends on the putting green. Keep your stats.

4. **Expect to get better.** After all, practice is just playing in small pieces. When you put it all together, your score will go down.

I have to get results fast. I coach high school kids. I get them for three months, tops, and only for a few hours a day, in between homework, school plays, student government, getting their driver's licenses, fighting acne, chasing the opposite sex, applying to college, working part-time, playing other sports, cutting the lawn, family vacations, and chasing the opposite sex. If our golf team is going to have a winning record, I have a couple weeks before the actual season starts to turn these wannabes into a team, a few practice matches to work on their games, and then eight league matches that determine our fate for the season and whether there'll be any postseason tournaments. If I'm real lucky, I get some of the same kids the next year.

So, if you want to lower your score in just a few weeks, I can help. I'll treat you like my high school players. That is, I'll treat you like someone who loves golf but has other things in your life. Like kids, pets, homes, husbands, wives, and careers (other than golf).

PLAN:
What We Won't Work On

We're not going to fiddle with your swing. I'm going to leave it alone. I'm going on the assumption that you take the club back in something that roughly resembles an arc, you bring it forward pretty much following the path of the backswing, you strike the ball, good or bad, each time you swing, and then your swing continues in a forward motion after you hit the ball until you finish with the club up in the air, pointing in one direction or another. I'm making this assumption because it's hard to get hooked on the game until you can hit the ball past your body just about every time you whack at it.

Okay, I'll give you one brief lesson in how to swing a golf club: Smooth.

We're not going to work on your grip, either. I figure if you can swing the club at the ball and make the ball travel in the direction of the hole, you're holding on to the club in a reasonable way. Unless the club keeps flying out of your hands (temper tantrums don't count), your grip is fine with me.

I don't care about your stance. (I might make an exception when we get into the short game.) I'm going on the same assumptions I did with swing and grip. You must be facing roughly in the right direction or the ball would be going the wrong direction. If you're off to the left, you know enough to turn right and vice versa. (Well, now you do.)

I also don't care about your shoes, your hat, your glove, or your clubs. Your shoes ought to fit and have spikes so you don't twirl around like a ballerina in the sand. Your hat should have somebody's logo on it because all hats these days have somebody's logo. You should wear a glove if your hand hurts or the club slips and not if you don't need it (though it does look pretty cool to leave a glove hanging out of your back pocket when you stop to get a cold drink at the turn). And, as for clubs, I prefer the kind with shafts and heads. There are all kinds of clubs and frankly, some are better than others. Wooden heads, aluminum heads, hollow, solid, lighter, heavier, metal, fiberglass, whippier shafts, stiffer shafts, aerodynamic, bionic, psychic, endorsed by Klingons, you name it. You have to find the clubs that feel right for you. And feel is everything, so I wouldn't presume to tell you what feels best in your hands.

PLAN:
What We Will Work On

Crosby's Five

So-named because there are five of them and my name is Crosby. Simple, like my whole approach to the game.

Crosby One—The Practice Range
Good for two shots off your game.

Anybody can tell you to practice. (Anybody who's ever heard a kid torture a violin knows some practice sessions have better results than others.) I'll show you *how* to practice. It doesn't do you any good to go out to the range and keep repeating bad habits. I'll show you how to practice what's good and stop doing what's bad.

Each time you practice, you should see improvement. If you don't, reread the practice section of this book or try a new range. The one you're going to is bad luck.

Crosby Two—The Short Game
Another two to three shots off your score.

A drive, a fairway wood and/or a middle iron and you're near the green, but it takes you three or four more shots to get in the hole. Why? You just sent the ball two or three hundred yards in two or three (even four) shots, and now it takes you as many to go fifty yards. Chip shots should save your score, not threaten it. Don't worry. They're easy to fix. And so are sand shots. Yes, sand shots. It's all in your head. If we played the whole game of golf on sand and sometimes hit the ball into a grass trap, we'd all have mental blocks about grass.

Crosby Three—Putting
Imagine no three-putt greens. How many shots would that save you?

Most golfers are better hitters than putters. That's because hitting is about motion and putting is about thinking. And thinking screws up everything. (Why do you think miniature golf is so hard? All those windmills to worry about.) Don't worry. Putting is a motion, just like hitting, only softer. I'll have you not thinking in no time. And putting much better.

Crosby Four—The Golf Course
A golf course you know is two shots easier than one you don't.

Most people play the same course every week. But they don't know the course. They don't know, in advance, approximately how far it is to the green from where their tee shot lands, even though it lands in that general area nearly every time they play. They don't think ahead about where to hit their approach shot depending on the slope of the green. And if they don't think about these things on their home course, imagine what they don't know about a new course. And it's so easy to find out. You can look (and play) so smart just by giving yourself a little course in "course."

Crosby Five—Stats
You can't get better unless you're know how you're doing.

How many shots does it take you, on average, to get near the green on a par four? How many putts per green do you take? Do you have more pars than bogies? More double bogies than bogies? Do you play long holes better than short holes? I'll show you how to identify your own strengths and weaknesses so you know what needs work and what just needs to stay as it is.

Expect Results

Each of Crosby's Five is good for one to three shots per round, which adds up to about ten strokes off your score.

Five for ten. That's a pretty good deal.

CROSBY ONE

It's not a driving range.
It's a practice range.

EVEN BEFORE HE WAS ON THE TEAM, TIGER HELPED ME TEACH THE FIRST LESSON OF GOLF: PRACTICE, PRACTICE, PRACTICE

The first time I ever saw or even heard of Tiger Woods was one night when my family was watching the old TV show *That's Incredible.* It was a ritual in our house, partly because my wife's sister was married to the producer. We sort of gave my brother-in-law credit for finding all the amazing stuff—the couple who got married while skydiving, a house that melted in the desert, a family of eighteen whose names all started with the letter *R*, a dog that used the bathroom and flushed the toilet.

Anyway, one night I saw this little kid, maybe nine years old, sitting on Fran Tarkenton's lap and talking golf. Well, I've been a golf nut for years, so just seeing a little kid who could talk the game like he could—"tee it low into the wind" and "open the club face for more loft"—well, I thought, yeah, "that's incredible." They had this tee set up on the stage, and the kid got up and started hitting golf balls into a net. They were gauging the distance: 200 yards! 225! He was nine years old. His swing was picture-perfect. Fran Tarkenton, who isn't too bad an all-around athlete, had his mouth hanging open. He said the kid's name was Tiger Woods and he'd been swinging a club since he was an infant. An infant?! I said to my wife, "Tiger's not a name you forget. We're gonna hear about that little boy."

Then, sure enough, in the late eighties I started seeing Tiger's name pop up in junior tournaments. (I must have coach's blood in me. I can't read a sports section without searching for the articles about youngsters, sandlots, Little League, YMCAs . . . those tiny back-page stories about some fourteen-year-old Pony League pitcher who threw four shutout innings. I find that stuff way more interesting than how the 49ers crushed some other NFL team in Super Bowl Whatever Number.) So, I'd see Tiger in this tournament or that one. He was only twelve or thirteen, but his scores just kept getting lower.

Then he won the Optimist International Junior World Championship down in San Diego. They picked up that story and ran it all over the place. I had friends back East telling me they'd heard of this prodigy named Tiger.

About that same time, I had the kids on my golf team working in the golf-cart barn at the navy-base course in Los Alamitos. Unlike a lot of the players at competing schools, our kids' families don't belong to country clubs where they can just sign their name, walk on, and play. Every time my guys want to play golf, they have to pay greens fees at a public course, and that's not money their families want to shell out too often. So, I find them these jobs at golf courses where they get to play and practice for free. And they get one other perk. They can take a guest with them . . . their devoted coach, me.

In '88 and '89 the navy course was like a private country club for Western High's team and me. I'd call up one of my guys and say, "Hey, I want to see your tee shots (or your fairway irons or how you blast out of the sand)." So we got to play . . . without having to join the navy.

It seems like every time we were there, there was this kid pounding balls at the range. He was probably in the sixth or seventh grade. Somebody told us that was Tiger Woods. He was this little guy, maybe five feet tall in golf spikes, and no more than eighty pounds. It was hard to believe he could be so good—until you saw him swing a club.

Tiger was usually on the practice tee before we got there and still there after we played nine holes in the afternoon. He might be hitting woods and long irons off the tee, a hundred shots or more. Or he'd drop a bucket of balls around the green and chip, chip, chip, backspin and bite. Or he'd putt, starting with long ones that break every which way and working his way down to gimmes.

Tiger would just practice, practice, practice. Meanwhile, my guys wanted to play, play, play.

I'd say, "You've got to practice before you play." And they'd say, "Playing is practicing." I'd say, "No, when you play, you only get one try at that four-iron at the turn of the dogleg. Maybe two tries if there's nobody playing behind you. On the practice tee, you can hit forty of them."

> **Playing isn't practicing. Practicing is practicing.**

Over and over, I'd repeat my Practice Routine mantra:

A dozen shots with each club. From the driver through the rest of the woods, from the long irons to the middle irons. Open the face, close the face. Tee it forward, tee it dead center, tee it back. Then the short game. A dozen shots from a hundred yards off the green, a dozen from seventy-five yards, a dozen from fifty, a dozen from twenty-five. Finally putting. From fifteen-footers down to twelve-inchers.

They'd give me that look that kids give adults, swear to me they'd practice but right now, *please* could we play?

So, we'd play. But we kept passing Tiger on the range on our way to the first tee and passing him on the range on our way back from the last hole. Little by little, they noticed. Look how good he is. Look how much he practices. Tiger was methodical; he hit shot after shot, club after club, through his whole bag. Then, if it was still light out, he started over. He had a Practice Routine, just like the coach was always harping about. Finally that image even made a dent in the concrete minds of my guys. Especially when they came in from a lousy round.

Play, play, play equals not so good. Practice, practice, practice equals improvement. Maybe this Tiger kid was onto something.

One day I came out to the course and, instead of finding the guys waiting to tee off, I found them whacking balls on the practice range. That's when I knew something was sinking in. Thanks, Tiger. You helped me teach my first lesson before you were even on the team.

One day in 1990, my number-one player casually said to me, "Coach, Tiger Woods lives in my neighborhood." I stopped cold. "Same housing tract as you?" I said, afraid to even think what I'm thinking. "Yeah," he said, "he lives right around the corner from me." "Same Tiger Woods we saw at Los Alamitos, not some other kid coincidentally named Tiger Woods?" I asked, just to make sure this wasn't some kind of cruel joke. "Yeah, coach, *the* Tiger Woods." Well, he might just as well have told me Johnny Unitas, Mickey Mantle, and Michael Jordan were going to play for Western High. This was a coach's dream . . .

. . . that could turn into a nightmare. In the late eighties and early nineties our entire school district was experiencing declining enrollment. Teachers were getting "riffed," another way of saying "fired," boundaries were constantly getting adjusted to keep the schools about the same size, junior highs were closing altogether, and Western High bounced from a three-year to a four-year school. My fear was that Tiger's street would get adjusted right out of Western's boundary and into some other school's.

Every June, when we'd sign out for the summer, we'd go see our principal, Craig Haugen, to talk about how the past year had gone and what we expected for the next year. For a couple of consecutive Junes, I went into his office and pointed to this little square on the map on his wall and said, "This little square over here, that's in Cypress, and that's where the future best golfer in the world lives. So, if they start messing with our boundaries, you can give away anything but hold on to that little square, the square that has the best golfer in the world."

I don't know if Craig ever had to fight for it, or if he traded two streets for one, or if the boundaries got so convoluted they looked like snakes mating. But I do know that Tiger Woods got up on the morning of the first day of his freshman year of high school, walked out of his house, and out of his little square, right into Western High School. And I was one happy coach.

INSIGHT:
Two One-Hour Practice Sessions
Will Do More for Your Game Than the Same
Two Hours Spent Playing Nine Holes

Did you ever wonder how Tiger Woods hits so many lucky shots? Simple. He practices more than he plays. When he plays, he's already hit that amazing-perfect-impossible-lucky-miraculous shot a hundred times on the practice range.

Look at it logically. Say you can slip out of work early or get away from the house one day a week so you can get an extra nine holes in before the weekend. You feel like you got in some extra practice, right? Whoa.

How much practice did you really get? Let's assume you shoot 48 for nine holes. If you two-putt six greens, three-putt two, and one-putt one, that leaves twenty-nine shots. There's bound to be a par three, maybe two, on the course, so you only get seven or eight tee shots, probably only half of which call for a driver. You get only four chances to hit your driver. Only three to hit your three- or four-wood off the tee. And now you're down to twenty-two shots. How many fairway woods do you hit? One on the par five, maybe another one on a long par four. Two fairway woods in nine holes! That's all. And twenty remaining shots to divide between your two-, three-, four-, five-, six-, seven-, eight-, and nine-iron and your wedge. That's 2.2 shots per club. *You average two shots per club in your bag in a whole round of practice!* Is that practice? Hardly. That's just a chance to see your mistakes and curse forty-eight times.

Now, take the same two hours and really practice—twice a week, an hour each time.

LESSON:
The Sixty-Minute Miracle

Here's how it works. Get a bucket of balls—approximately 120 balls. Take them out to the practice range. *Hold it! Don't touch the balls. Don't hit anything.*

First, Get Ready to Get Ready

Stretch. Put your left arm across your chest, grab it at the elbow with your right hand, and pull. Do it three or four times. Then do the other arm.

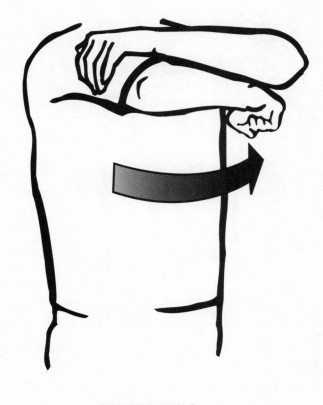

STRETCHING

Pivot. Just plant your feet and coil your hips like you're in your backswing, then uncoil as if you're swinging through. Do that three times. (If you're young, that should do it. If you're older like me, stretch until you feel loose, or until the sun goes down, whichever comes first.)

Swing two clubs together. Take out your three-iron. Don't hit anything! Take out your five-iron, too. Hold both clubs and swing them slowly. You know, like a designated hitter in baseball warms up in the on-deck circle. The key thing is, swing slowly. Imagine you're in slow motion, like in a movie. Swing twenty times that way until you're in a groove that feels perfect. Same swing, real slow, over and over.

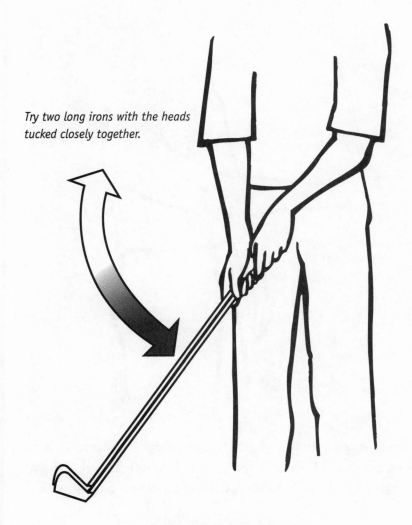

Try two long irons with the heads tucked closely together.

TWO-CLUB SWING

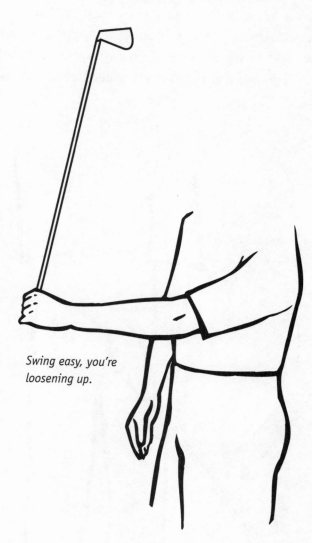

*Swing easy, you're
loosening up.*

One-handed swing. Another good warm-up exercise is to
swing one club, like your driver, using only your left hand, if you're
right-handed. (If you're left-handed . . . I don't have to explain this,
do I?)

Get Ready

A dozen balls. Okay, you're almost ready to hit. Count out twelve balls. No more, no less. And do NOT start in with your driver. Remember how I said I wasn't going to work on your swing? Well, I lied. I'm not going to change it or adjust it but I am going to show you how to "build your swing." Most golfers go to the range and start with the biggest club they have, the driver. (I think it's because they get to set the ball up on a tee where they figure it's harder to miss it altogether.) Then, they go down through other clubs—three-wood, four-wood, five, then from the long to the short irons. Wrong! Start small—a gentle half-swing, then a three-quarter-swing—until you build up to a full swing. Same groove, same motion, same rhythm. Just increase the arc, the thrust, and the follow-through. Adding is easier than subtracting.

Aim. Now you're just about ready to hit golf balls. But before you do, aim at something. Golf is a game of *aiming* at a target, whether it's a fairway, a green, a flag, or a hole. But people on a practice range, and even on a course, forget that. They hit toward the open space, which on a range can be a hundred yards wide, a lot wider than most any fairway you'll play. Why are ranges so wide? Money. The wider the range, the more golfers side by side, hitting bucket after bucket of golf balls. What you have to do is *create your own fairway.* Pick two objects—shrubs, trees, mounds, yard markers, brown spots, whatever—and make them your boundaries. Don't be unrealistic and pick two bushes six feet apart. Try your best to eyeball about twenty to thirty yards.

IMAGINARY FAIRWAY ON PRACTICE RANGE

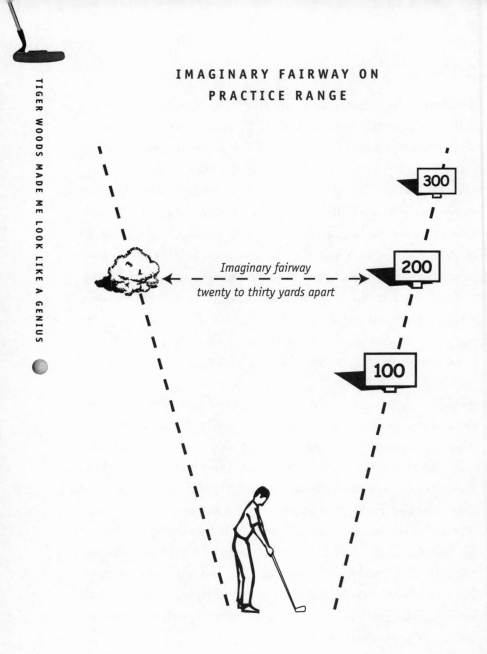

Imaginary fairway twenty to thirty yards apart

300

200

100

All right, believe it or not, now you're ready to hit golf balls.

Every Other Club

1. Half wedges. Start with your pitching wedge. Pick a spot in your imaginary fairway for an imaginary green, say about fifty or sixty yards out. There may not be a fifty-yard marker on your practice range but there's always one at one hundred yards. (I guess I don't need to tell you to aim halfway.) Take a practice swing. Or rather, half of a practice swing. Imagine a full circle around your body. You're going to use half of it. Take the club back to about waist high, swing gently through, and finish about waist high. Check the Swing Circle diagram on the following page to find your backswing and follow-through position for each club, starting with the half-wedge.

Now drop a ball about midway between your feet. Look at your target on the fairway. Fix that image in your mind. Step up and shift your focus from the target to the ball. (Once you have the image of where you're hitting fixed in your mind, you have no reason to look up at your target until you've finished hitting.) Now just think slow and gentle . . . and hit a half-wedge. Watch where the ball lands. Did you come close to your target? Did you hit your imaginary green? **Hit twelve half wedges.** Adjust logically after each one. Do you need to aim more left of right? Are you falling short or overshooting so you need to increase or decrease your arc? Common sense will fix 90 percent of all golf mistakes. When you hit one the way you wanted, just try to imitate yourself. Slow and gentle.

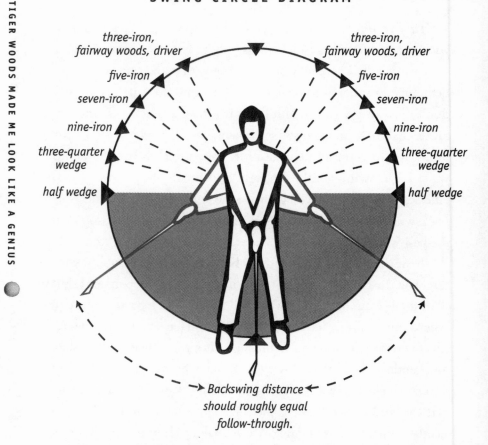

three-iron,
fairway woods, driver

three-iron,
fairway woods, driver

five-iron

five-iron

seven-iron

seven-iron

nine-iron

nine-iron

three-quarter
wedge

three-quarter
wedge

half wedge

half wedge

➤ Backswing distance ←
should roughly equal
follow-through.

**Arcs of three-quarter wedge, half wedge, nine-, seven-,
five-, and three-irons, and woods.**

2. Next, ***three-quarter wedges.*** They're just a little bigger version of the half wedges. Your backswing takes your hands to shoulder height; swing through slow and gentle; and finish again with your hands at shoulder height. As you'll see in the Swing Circle, the three-quarter wedge is the same kind of swing as the half wedge with a little added to the arc at either end.

Aim for a target about sixty to ninety yards out—whatever fits your game. **Hit twelve three-quarter wedges.** Assess. Adjust.

Swing easy. (As you'll see, I believe you can get the biggest results from the smallest shots.)

3. *Nine-irons.* Take twelve more balls out of the bucket. Uh-uh. No more. Just twelve. Look down your imaginary fairway toward the hundred-yard marker, approximate how far *you* hit a nine-iron, and aim for a target about that far—probably from 90 to 130 yards. Or, if your range is like a lot of them these days, it has greens placed around and usually has one about 120 yards out that you can use as a gauge.

And we continue building your swing. As you'll see in the Swing Circle, with the nine-iron you want to use about two-thirds of the circle. Take a practice swing where you bring the club back so your hands are just above shoulder height, swing through, and finish with your hands again just above shoulder height.

Put a ball down between your feet. Look at your target. Fix it in your mind. Then step up to the ball, change your focus from the target to the ball, think slow and gentle, backswing and finish. How'd you do? Left? Right? Short or long? You know what to do. Adjust. Use logic. Try again. **Hit twelve nine-irons.** Aim in or out. Add or decrease your arc. You can even experiment with moving the ball forward or backward in your stance. The closer the ball is to your front foot, the greater loft and less distance you'll get, and the reverse is true the closer it is to your back foot.

4. No, not eight-irons. ***Seven-irons.*** Skip every other club in your bag every other time you practice. Nine-iron, seven, five, and three, then every other wood. That way you cover the spectrum of distances and you get enough practice with each club every time you practice. It also keeps you from getting bored by doing the exact same thing over and over.

Okay, same routine with the seven as with nine. Approximate how far you hit a seven-iron—probably in the area of 120 to 155 yards. Then use the 150 marker as your gauge.

As for your swing with the seven, first look at the Swing Circle around your body. This time you're going to use up all but about 20 percent of the whole circle. Take a practice swing, bringing the club back to where your hands are about two hands higher than your shoulders, swing through, and finish with your hands the same distance above your shoulders. I don't have to tell you to hit the ball harder, because you're going to. By adding to the arc, you're adding speed, and speed will add force. So don't consciously hit any harder. There's no need. Try a couple more practice swings.

Now **hit twelve seven-irons.** Check your results. Compensate. Use common sense. Adjust yourself.

5. Five-irons. Approximate your distance. Find a target in your imaginary fairway. Take a practice swing. Only now, as you can see in the Swing Circle, you're using most of the arc, a full swing. Take the club back to the point where your hands are above your right shoulder, swing through, and finish in the same position on the other side.

Hit your twelve five-irons. Once again, don't hit harder. The club will do it for you, naturally. If you come up short of your target, then you might add a little oomph. Or take some off if you're over-shooting the target. But you're better off to the *let the ball go the distance it wants to* with the particular club, learn it, and just hit the club that fits the situation.

6. Three-irons. Same as the five. Check the Swing Circle. Again, you're using the full arc, or almost the full arc. The longer the club, the more difficult it may be to gauge how far you hit that club. Just experiment. Don't change your swing; change your target to fit the distance the ball wants to go with that club.

Hit twelve three-irons. Fix the target in your mind, then shift your focus to the ball. Check your results. Keep the ball in your imaginary fairway. Always aim for your target. Adjust, hit, adjust, hit.

TECHNIQUE:
The Railroad Tracks Trick

A helpful tip, no matter what club you're hitting, is to think of railroad tracks running from the tee to the target. Lay a club down in front of your feet to be the inside rail. An imaginary line from the ball to the target creates the outside rail. Adjust the line of the club and your feet so they're parallel with the outside rail. Now your feet and body are aimed *left* of the target while the ball and the hitting arc are aimed *at* the target. Too many golfers aim their bodies and feet at the target, so the ball and hitting arc end up aimed to the right of the target.

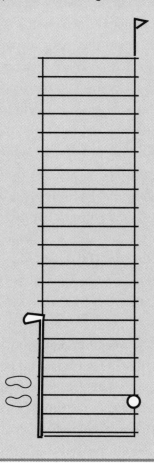

TIME OUT: It's okay to stop between shots or clubs. In fact, it's important. Take a step back from where you're hitting and look at where your balls are clustered out on the range. Are they getting better or worse? Further left or right? Loosen up. Just stop and breathe. Admire your good shots. Think about how you can alter things for your not-so-good ones. But just plain taking a break and assessing things is good. Golf never was a fast game. So slow down. Good golfers are relaxed.

7. Okay, time for the *fairway woods*. We'll start with the five-wood. Figure you'll hit it about 175 to 220, adjusting for your own game. Find the 200-yard marker and estimate from there.

Now it's more important than ever to picture that imaginary fairway, because this is a fairway wood. Pick out your target, the big tree or the rise or whatever. Stare at it a few seconds and burn it into your mind. You can hit a target much better if it's in your mind even when you're not looking right at it.

Now **hit twelve fairway woods.** Imagine you're out on the course, in the fairway, and you're using the five-wood to get you up next to the green. That big tree on the range is the green. Take a full swing. As the Swing Circle shows, that means your hands will cover about 320 degrees of a 360-degree circle. Or, if you think of a clock, they'll go from the numeral one to the numeral eleven. And don't forget, you shouldn't have to hit hard or soft. Just relax and let the ball go as far as it wants to go with that club. Then adjust.

8. *The driver.* You've been hitting about forty-five minutes by this point, including a few breaks to size up your progress, assess, change, and occasionally admire a really great shot. Now you finally get to hit the club most golfers start with. The driver. With the ball propped up on tee. Oh boy. You can let it all out and sock the day-lights out of it, right? Yes. (Surprised you, didn't I?)

See, you're going to hit with all you've got without even trying. Because, club by club, you've been working up to it. You started easy with a half-swing and worked your way around the degrees of the circle to the point where a full swing off a tee is just the next natural step. You'll find when you practice in this progression, each club will seem easier to hit. You'll be ready for it instead of drawing on all your energy at the beginning of a practice session and expending too much up front.

Hit twelve drives. You know the drill by now. Create the fairway. Find the target. Fix it in your mind. Step up to the ball. Swing. Adjust. Swing. Did you notice how easy the swing came? How the arc was natural and relaxed? How far the ball traveled without your having to try too hard? That's because you "built" your swing, club by club.

9. Extra credit. Okay, you hit half-wedges, three-quarter wedges, nine-, seven-, five-, and three-irons, the five-wood and your driver. Twelve shots each. That's ninety-six shots. You should have several balls left in the bucket. **Hit any club you think needs extra work.** Go to the five-iron, for instance, reset your arc and your target, and swing away.

> **HINT: Finish where you started.** If you still have a few balls left, hit half or three-quarter wedges. It's almost like a cooldown exercise. You end with small shots, gentle shots, leaving your game with finesse instead of power and emphasizing the part of the game that will ultimately cut the most strokes off your score. (See Crosby Two.)

That was your first practice session. Next time you'll still start with half and three-quarter wedges, but then you'll go to the eight-, six-, four-, and two-irons . . . or a seven-wood[1], then the three-wood, and you'll still finish with the driver.

You just hit 120 golf balls in an hour and got more out of each club than you could in three or four nine-hole rounds. If you can get out to the range twice a week, come the weekend, you'll have hit every club in your bag at least twelve times, not to mention twenty-four wedges and drives.

RESULTS:
A.K.A. Miracles

The very next round you play, you'll notice several things:

- Your swing will be ready. You've been building it every time you practice.

- You'll have a sense of how far each club will take the ball. You won't have to overswing, hit too hard, or just guess wrong about which club to hit.

- More shots will seem familiar. When you walk up to your ball in the fairway, you'll realize you've already hit virtually the same five-iron shot twelve times this week. This is just another one.

- You'll develop good habits. Like aiming. Fixing the target in your mind. Shifting your focus from the target to the ball.

- You'll hit a lot more "lucky" shots, like Tiger Woods, because you'll have already hit a shot a lot like that lucky one. It only looks lucky to the others in your foursome who didn't get out to the practice range.

---

1. If you're like a lot of golfers today, you don't hit a two-iron anymore. (And the old joke is that nobody but Jack Nicklaus and God can hit a one-iron.) I've replaced my two-iron with a seven-wood. I like the loft, and I'd rather hit the seven-wood from the fairway.

Sometimes Even Tiger
Couldn't Resist Playing

After practicing and practicing, you're bound to want to see if you're making progress. Am I really getting better? How much better? How would I do on a really tough challenge? Sometimes the temptation to test yourself is just too much to resist.

Back in Tiger's sophomore year, we played in a tournament that I helped run in Monterey at Rancho Canada. Some of the best teams in California were there. Tiger set the all-time tournament record—only one over for two days, playing one day on the East course and the next on the West. The whole team rose to the occasion, and we finished fifth in the tournament. After that, the kids wanted to unwind.

We'd driven up in my motor home, all our gear and clubs and players piled into the back. On the way home, I took the famous Seventeen-Mile Drive, which just happened to take us past Cypress Point, the very well-known, very private club. I'm not sure if it was my idea or the kids', but they were all dying to say they'd played Cypress, especially Tiger. So I pulled off the road near the 15th tee, the team hopped the fence, and I handed their clubs over. The plan was, they'd play 15, 16, and 17, I'd pick them up near the 18th tee, and we'd get out of there before anyone knew better.

Everything started off fine. They played number 15, a par-three over water. Then they went to the 16th, the world-famous, breathtaking 220-yard hole over the ocean that everyone has seen on television. While they played, I drove the motor home down to Seal Point, near the 17th green, for our rendezvous. The problem was, the team got caught just as Tiger was about to hit his tee shot. It seems we weren't the only trespassers ever to get the idea of sneaking onto Cypress. The team was escorted right off the course.

Meanwhile, I was waiting down the road, wondering how it could take so long to play two more holes. Finally, I saw them walking up the road, carrying their clubs, and I figured their three-hole round had been cut short. Still, they said it was worth it.

I wonder if anyone at Cypress realized they had the distinction of kicking Tiger Woods off their golf course.

Crosby's Quick Refresher
CROSBY ONE—PRACTICING

Playing isn't practicing. Practicing is practicing. There are no lucky shots, just more familiar ones.

LESSON: The Sixty-Minute Miracle
An hour on the practice range

1. **Get ready to get ready**—Stretch, pivot, swing with two clubs, swing one-handed.

2. **Get ready**—"Build" your swing from short clubs to long
   - Aim: create your own (mental) fairway on practice range.

3. **Hit every other club**—A dozen shots per club
   - Half wedge, three-quarter wedge, nine-iron, seven, five, three, then woods.
   - Next time alternate—eight-iron, six, four, two, etc.
   - Cool down—finish on club you started with.

4. **Use Swing Circle**—Imagine hitting inside a circle, adjust arc per club—i.e. backswing to hips and follow through to hips, backswing to shoulders and follow through to shoulders, etc.

TECHNIQUE: The Railroad Tracks Trick
For better aim, lay down a club in front of feet, toward fairway, and imagine a path disappearing in the distance like railroad tracks.

RESULTS: Expect them. Practice works.

CROSBY TWO

The shortcut to a lower score
is in the last hundred yards.

Right now you're saying, didn't we cover pitching and chipping when we were at the practice range? No. That's practicing hitting each club, knowing its distance limitations, how to adjust left or right, getting your swing in a groove. On the practice range you aim for an area, say two hundred yards out, around what would be the middle of the fairway, or seventy-five yards out, just off the front of the where the green might be. When you practice your short game, you're aiming for a spot, not an area. The spot is the part of the green where the hole sits or, ideally, the hole itself. Think of pitching—approach shots to the green—as landing the ball as close to the cup as possible. Think of chipping—shots from the edge of the green—as putting, only in the air. Once the ball goes in the hole, your score stops getting any higher. That's the whole idea of the game of golf.

Improving your short game is the fastest, easiest, surest way to get better at golf. It's the way to beat a player who seems better than you, one who hits longer and straighter. It's the way to lower your handicap without quitting your day job and turning your life savings over to a touring pro for lessons.

But most players take pitching and chipping for granted. Maybe it's because we refer to those shots in such diminutive terms. It's a "chip," not a "hit." A "pitch," not a "throw." A "wedge," not a "wood." But those are the biggest little shots in golf. Why get the ball to the edge of the green in one or two and then take four more to get it in the hole? That's just plain inefficient.

Once you get inside one hundred yards—one football field from the green—you aren't playing the tail end of a par 4 or 5; you're playing a short par 3. You have to be able to make par inside that last hundred yards. You have to play with confidence, and the only way you get confidence is when things are routine instead of brand new.

Like a Broadway performer, rehearse, rehearse, rehearse. Actors would all die of stage fright if they didn't rehearse the show to an empty house for weeks, then take it out on the road for a few months, tinker with it, and take it from the top all over again before opening night. By the time *Cats* became the longest-running show on Broadway, it hadn't gotten old, it had gotten better. Don't ever think you get stale with rehearsal. You just get better because you know what to expect.

If you want to play with confidence, you have to experiment when it doesn't count, get the mistakes out of your system, and start to hone and perfect the desired performance. Work your way toward the right club, the right loft, the right arc, the right follow-through, and then do it over and over (and over and over and over . . .). Just like the cast of *Cats*.

By the way, as you'll see later, putting is like chipping, only more so. By that I mean there are even fewer variables. No high grass. No sand. Almost no wind. Just distance, roll, and green speed. It's all in the stroke. If you have to make three inside of a hundred yards, then you have to get down in one or two once you're on the green. (I'll cover putting in Crosby Three.)

MAGIC, OR, TIGER'S DISAPPEARING BALL TRICK

You know those shots that look like magic you see in tournaments on TV, like when the pro swings through waist-high weeds in the rough and the ball rolls up four feet from the pin, or when he blasts out of a sand trap the size of the D-Day beach at Normandy and holes out the shot? What if I told you I had found out the secret the pros use, that I knew how they make those magic shots?

Well, I do know. And I'm going to let you in on the secret. There's no such thing as magic. Magicians don't practice magic; they practice making things *look* like magic. So do golf pros. The key word, once again, is *practice*. Those shots are anticipated difficulties that the pros work on, in advance, so they're ready for them when they occur. I know. I teach that same secret to my players. Practice makes magic.

I watched Tiger turn practice into magic for four years. When he was a senior, I took the team up to Canada around Easter time. We were playing in a tournament against two Canadian schools at a resort called Olympic View Golf Course. The resort people had been very hospitable to us the summer before, and now they were letting us take seven kids up to play against the two local teams. It gave us the experience of the trip, the competition, and the chance to practice and play on an extraordinary golf course.

A few days before the tournament, we were out on the course, I believe it was a Sunday, and I happened to be playing with Tiger. Most often, I had him playing with some of the other kids so they could learn from his example, but in the rotation he just happened to be playing with me that day (and, though I didn't know it then, providing me material to someday put in my book). This incident will give you an insight into how Tiger and other great players seem to come up with crucial shots just when they need them.

We were practicing late in the afternoon, and by this time we were on the 5th or 6th hole. Tiger was out there to practice more than play, so he was constantly stopping somewhere and saying, "Coach, wait a minute." Then he'd grab a club, walk to a particular spot, drop some extra balls, and start hitting. You see, he'd be thinking as he was walking the course about where he might end up after a tee shot or a second shot. He'd be on the left edge of the fairway and think, "The way I hit my drives, I could easily be right here." So he'd drop extra balls and hit them from there. Or he'd get up near the green and just stop and look at the hole from there. He was thinking again, "The way I seem to play this hole, my second shot could put me right here, and then what would I do?" He didn't want to wonder when the game was for real. He wanted to be ready.

In this instance, he grabbed his lob wedge, walked about twenty feet off the green to the spot he'd picked out, and dropped down six balls. This spot was up a slight slope, maybe four or five feet above the putting surface, with the grass about two or three inches high. He was going to pitch the balls downhill, toward the pin, from the high side of the green. I watched all this intently, watched his mind size up a situation that hadn't even occurred yet. I studied him studying the course. Tiger looked at the pin, opened his club up real wide, laid it totally open the way you now see him do on TV. And then he hit this big lob shot, almost straight up in the air, trying to get it to stop right near the cup. I'd say he hit three balls, and not one came close to where he wanted them. Oh, they were good chip shots, rolling close enough that he might one-putt. But they didn't threaten to drop in.

So, he took three more. He fiddled with how much the club face was open and got the next three a little closer to the hole. He stood there and absorbed it all, and then went on to the next hole. You could see he was figuring out how to get that ball closer and closer to the hole when and if he should be playing from that spot, or a spot like it, around that green or another similar one.

We all practiced a couple more rounds and finally got to the tournament. By the last day of the match, we'd built up quite a crowd watching us, "us" being another way of saying Tiger. At the last hole, it was kind of a miniature version of the end of the U.S. Open, with a ring of fans five deep around the green as we came up the fairway. The last hole was a 530-yard par-5, and Tiger's second shot was even with the pin but left of the green. The pin was maybe ten feet into the green, and his ball was about fifteen or sixteen feet off the green. But here's the critical information. His ball was up about four feet above the hole, and the grass was two or three inches tall, just like it was on the hole where he had practiced. Nobody in that whole crowd but me knew Tiger was about to hit a shot he'd hit over and over and over a few days before—club face open, high loft, backspin, and a slow roll toward the pin. I was standing at the back of the green studying the shot before Tiger got there. They even had television coverage at the last hole, and the cameras were pointed at Tiger as he walked up the slope toward his ball. This Canadian fan who was standing right next to me said, "Well, this is an impossible shot. He'll be lucky to keep it on the green."

I should have just nodded and agreed with him about how tough the shot was, but I couldn't resist. I said, "It'll be on the green." This guy looked at me like I was dreaming and said, "What?" I just couldn't stop myself; I replied, "You won't believe how good he is at these shots." The Canadian guy rolled his eyes at this American having delusions.

That day was the first time I consciously wondered if Tiger actually plays better when he's surrounded by crowds and cameras. Coaches and sportswriters say that's the difference between good and great, whether it's a PGA golfer who stands over a forty-footer, an NBA shooting guard who puts up a three-pointer at the buzzer, or an Olympic gymnast who has to get all 9.5s or better to win the gold. The great ones get better when you turn up the heat. (Just think if the rest of us could respond to pressure by performing better.) Of course, these days there's no question, Tiger definitely takes his game up a notch when he's on the spot. The bigger the troop that follows him up the fairway, the louder the cheers he hears from another hole, the more hushed the crowd around the green, the greater the tension in the air, the more chance there is that Tiger Woods is going to reach in his bag for a club and pull out a rabbit.

Back to this shot on the 18th. Remember, he had hit six practice shots the earlier day and they were all respectable shots, but that time, when I was watching him, none got any closer than a foot or two. Now, he had six hundred people watching, cameras running, reporters reporting, and kids hopping up and down to see over grownups. Tiger looked at the shot, mentally calculating the distance to the pin and the slope down to the hole. Then he rolled the face of his wedge wide open, took the club back, swung through the high grass, hit the ball almost ninety degrees straight up, backspinning all the way. Finally, it dropped and seemed like it was stopping at a red light four feet from the hole. Then it rolled down, curved a little, first left, then right, as if it were following a street map, and, *plunk*, it dropped into the cup for an eagle. Tiger raised his fist up in victory, loving that moment. I loved that moment. The Canadian guy looked at me with this "How'd you know?" expression, thinking he must be standing next to the ghost of Ben Hogan's private instructor, and mumbled, "Wow! What a lucky shot!"

Wrong! It was a great shot, not a lucky one. Tiger had reduced the odds against the shot before he hit it. He performed for the crowd because he had rehearsed. That's the lesson that you take away whether you're Tiger or just one of us mortals. Chip shots aren't something you have to pray for. They're predictable. There's only a certain amount of real estate around the green. There are only a few locations on the green for the pin. There are only so many places your ball can land and only so many shots you can face from there. Uphill with a lot of run. Over a bunker with loft and a little roll. Downhill with backspin and good brakes. Fifty feet, twenty feet, five feet. Practice what could possibly happen. Six shots from possibility A, six from B, six from C, and so on. See what works and what doesn't. Adjust. Do six more from each position. The next time you play a round, an interesting thing will occur. One or more of those possibilities you practiced will actually happen. So you'll be hitting a shot you already know how to hit instead of one you have to pray for. Who knows, you might even play better with a little pressure on.

LESSON:
Pitching

Golf is like baseball. The better your pitching, the lower the score.

Get Comfortable. I told you we were going to find practical ways to lower your score. Practical means simple. So, I don't want you to get fancy with your short game. I want you to get familiar with it. I want you to get comfortable. I want you to learn pitching inside out, up and down, backswing, arc, and follow-through. Know that if you bring your wedge back to point A, the ball is going to travel X yards. If you bring it back to point B (let's say, a little farther than A), the ball is going to travel X + 10 or 20 or 30 yards. You just have to learn your individual As, Bs, Xs, and pluses.

The Power of the Short Game
a personal testimonial

Along with putting, your short game can save you more strokes than all the other shots combined. I'm living proof. Personally, there are lots of aspects of the game of golf where other guys can outperform me. Plenty of the kids on my golf teams can hit the ball off the tee farther than I can. Most of my weekend buddies can get more roll out of their "draw" shots. Some can pick a fairway wood out of high grass cleaner or hit the greens in regulation more often. But once we approach the greens, watch out. I know my way home from a hundred yards out better than Hansel and Gretel following bread crumbs. And I can't tell you how often I've outscored a bigger hitter once we get close enough that physical power doesn't matter.

The Pitching Clock

I should thank my daughter, April, for my short game (especially wedges), and anybody who's ever learned from me should thank her. When she was playing softball in high school and college, she was on travel teams and I went to her games religiously, every Saturday and Sunday. But even to a dedicated softball dad, those are the two most sacred days on the golf calendar. I'm pretty sure I was the only fan at the game who brought his shag bag, pitching wedge, and a little mat (so they wouldn't get mad at me for tearing up right field). I'd go out near the home run fence and hit one shot after another. Given the pace of the average softball game (they don't call it "slow-pitch" for nothing), I can safely say I never missed a key moment in my daughter's career while simultaneously improving my short game.

During a weekend, I would hit two to three hundred of those shots while I was watching my daughter play ball. The kids I coach know to listen to me when it comes to the short game. There isn't a distance I haven't hit so many times I could literally do it blindfolded. The goal is to gain the confidence of knowing that if you draw the club back to a given point, you'll hit the ball a certain distance, time and time again.

The pitching drill I teach is just what I did at the softball games. I'd hit forty-yard shots, fifty- and fifty-five-yard shots, sixties, seventies, all the way up to hundred-yard shots. And I hit dozens at each distance. This a drill I call the Pitching Clock, and here's how it works:

It's Eight P.M.
Do You Know Where Your Pitch Shot Is?

Imagine you're standing beside a clock dial. If you're right-handed, your back is to the numerals. If left-handed, you're facing the numerals.

PITCHING CLOCK

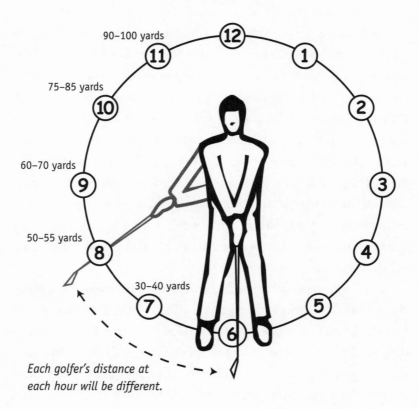

90–100 yards

75–85 yards

60–70 yards

50–55 yards

30–40 yards

Each golfer's distance at
each hour will be different.

Now, take the wedge back to just below waist level and hit the ball. That's about eight o'clock on the dial. Let's say it goes fifty yards. When it's eight o'clock, you hit the ball fifty yards. (Experiment until you find the fifty-yard point or "hour" as your base. Naturally, this varies from golfer to golfer.) Then, when you take your wedge back a few more degrees, say right up to waist level or nine o'clock, you'll add to your distance, probably five to ten yards. When it's nine o'clock, you may hit the ball fifty-five or sixty yards. Practice wedge shots with a back swing from eight o'clock to eleven o'clock. See how far you hit the ball from each "hour" to create a distance range from fifty all the way up to one hundred yards. Then pitch around the clock.

- **Seven o'clock.** Start by bringing the wedge back to your first clock point, say seven o'clock, and hit the ball about thirty to forty yards. (Remember, determine your individual backswing spots and resulting distances.) As soon as you hit a shot well from seven o'clock, try to **hit a dozen** just like the first one.

- **Eight o'clock.** Next, bring the club back to your second clock point, approximately eight o'clock, and hit the ball fifty to fifty-five yards. Now, try to **hit a dozen** like that.

- **Nine o'clock.** Okay, bring the club back to your next clock point, approximately nine o'clock on the dial, and then swing through, adding distance, so you're hitting somewhere between 60 and 70 yards. **Hit a dozen** taking your backswing to the same hour on your clock.

- **Ten o'clock.** Add an hour to your backswing and add still more distance. You should be hitting seventy-five to eighty-five yards. **Hit a dozen,** always aiming for the ball you hit first from that clock point.

- **Eleven o'clock.** Continue to take the club back further, now up to eleven o'clock, which should give you ninety to one hundred yards of distance. **Hit a dozen.**

Resetting your Clock—Corrections and Adjustments

Consistency. Is each of your shots going the same distance from the same point on the clock, or are some going fifty yards, some sixty-five, and some thirty? That's a matter of pace or speed of the swing. Just because you know the point on the clock where you want to stop doesn't mean you can jerk the club back there and jerk it forward and through the shot. You want to bring it back fairly slowly, take a little pause at the top, and then just release the club and follow through. Think of it like the relaxed rhythm of an old porch swing. Don't work too hard. Ease back—pause—release.

Accuracy. How close are your next ten shots coming to where you hit the first one or two at each "hour" on the clock? Realign your feet, left or right, to compensate for stray shots. Position the ball an inch or two closer to your front foot for more loft and a little less distance. Position it an inch or two closer to your back foot for less loft and more distance. Hit ten more shots with each adjustment, making them as routine as you can.

POSITION OF BALL TO FEET

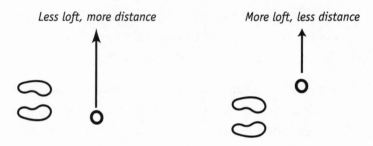

Less loft, more distance   *More loft, less distance*

Fine-tuning. How many yards are you adding with each additional "hour" of backswing? Let's say you're adding ten full yards when you go from eight to nine o'clock. Try splitting the difference, to a point halfway between eight and nine, until you only add about five yards to your shot, thereby adding accuracy to your short game. Each time you find a new clock point, hit ten to twelve more shots from that point.

Wind. When my kids are hitting a normal shot with a pitching wedge—relatively low wind, no trees or bushes to overcome, a green without too big a slope—I try to get them to hit the ball from about halfway between their feet. But if they're playing into the wind, we try to work on a "knockdown" shot, one that scoots under the wind. To do this you position the ball closer to your back foot.

At the same time, you think about keeping the club face closed and the club a little lower as you take it back to the "hour" you need, then release and follow through as you usually do. The geometry from that position sends the ball out at a lower trajectory.

PITCHING INTO WIND

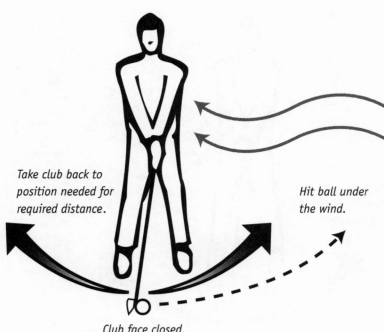

Take club back to position needed for required distance.

Hit ball under the wind.

Club face closed, ball position closer to back foot.

Lobbing. If you watch tennis matches, you know the value of a good lob shot. Instead of hitting the ball right at your problem (opponent, bush, tree, bunker, or sloping green), you lift the ball over your troubles. To hit the ball up high and stop it a little softer than normal, you do the opposite of the "knockdown" shot. Position the ball off your front foot, use an easy swing, and open up the club face a bit to give the ball more loft. Take the club back to the "hour" you need for distance, release, and follow through. You'll get a nice high arc and a helicopter set-down, a soft landing. If you've got a sharply sloping green, a shot like this will put the brakes on as it lands, like a helicopter. For even more loft, hit a sand wedge instead of a pitching wedge.

LOB SHOT

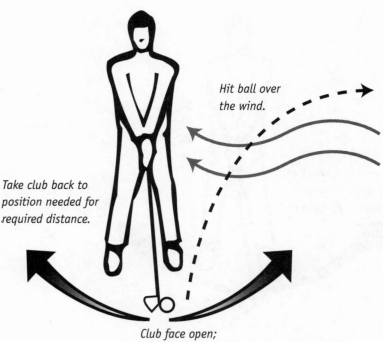

Hit ball over the wind.

Take club back to position needed for required distance.

Club face open; ball position closer to front foot.

If you don't have a daughter playing softball, go out in the backyard before work in the morning. (Or the local playground or high school field.) Put on headphones and listen to the news or a book on tape while you hit a half hour's worth of wedges. Hit another half hour's worth when you get home. In no time, you'll be hitting consistent wedges, and you'll have read a best-seller or two.

GAME:
Field Goal Golf

Field goals are three points. So are par 3s. Coincidence?

I always say, when you're inside that last hundred yards, think of it as a par 3 where you have to make par. The more control you have, the better your chance to par that hundred-yard hole. This next exercise is one Tiger and I invented on the football field to perfect that control. I call it "Field Goal Golf." When the football team wasn't practicing, we'd go out on the field with our wedges and "pitch" field goals. In other words, you drop a few balls down and try to hit them through the goalposts. If you split the uprights, you get three points or par.

FIELD GOAL GOLF

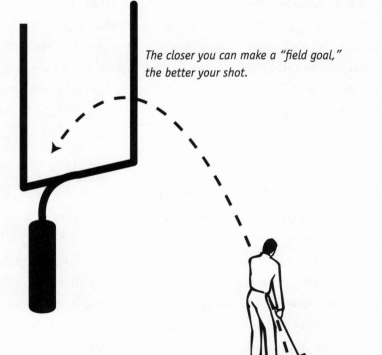

The closer you can make a "field goal," the better your shot.

But there is a key difference between field goal kicking and field goal pitching. In football, the farther you can kick the ball, the better you are. In golf, the closer you can stand to the uprights and still knock the ball over, the better you are. You can start with a pitching wedge, but to get really good and really close, you have to open up the face more and more, and move the ball further and further up in your stance. Eventually, to hit the ball almost straight up, you need the greater loft of a sand wedge.

Tiger would go out there and never even pick up the pitching wedge. He'd start with his sand wedge, and he'd stand pretty close to the goalposts, and then just get closer and closer. He'd hit the ball practically straight up in the air, through the uprights, and almost straight down on the other side.

Of course, Tiger was always competitive, so he would look for someone else on the team to pitch against. If another player could pitch it up and over from fifteen yards, Tiger would go for ten yards. If the other guy got one over at eight yards, Tiger wanted to do it from seven yards or five yards. One time, he got within four feet of the goalposts—a little over one yard—and he was hitting balls through, dropping them not more than five or six feet on the other side. Think about the control that can give you around the green.

LESSON:
Chipping away at Your Score

Once you get really close to the green, inside ten yards, you're moving from pitching to chipping. As I said earlier, a chip shot is like a putt, only airborne. It should be hit with the same care, finesse, and accuracy as a good putt. It should go for the hole and nothing less.

With chipping, we're going to work from the edge of the green outward, from the near fringe to the far fringe to off the fringe.

Wait! Why can't I putt from off the green?

It is true that the closer you are to the putting surface, the lower the club number you reach for. And it's true that since most of us have the greatest control with our putters, when the ball is just off the green, ideally, you want to reach for your putter. But ideally means only when you have ideal circumstances.

You can only chip with your putter when your situation meets the **three Ifs:**

If # 1: If the ball is close enough to the green.

If # 2: If the grass is short.

If # 3: If the ground is very nearly level.

TECHNIQUE:
The Three-Club Bag

When you're ten yards or less from the green, I teach what some people call the Three-Club Bag method: the six-iron, the eight-iron, and the pitching wedge. Learn the limits and possibilities of each of those three clubs. They can snatch a par from the jaws of a bogey.

Club 1—the six-iron hop-and-run. When the fourth "if" occurs, that is, the absence of any one of the first three (which is most of the time), it's time to reach for another club, starting with the six-iron. The six-iron is going to stay low and give you a lot of run and roll, like a putter with vitamins. So you have to be no more than four feet from the edge of the green. When you add on the distance to the pin at an average of fifteen to twenty feet, you have a total distance of nineteen to twenty-four feet, or about six to eight yards, no more. A well-aimed six-iron can be just what you need—a hop over the fringe, a couple of skips along the putting surface, and a steady roll toward the cup.

Since you're running the ball, read the green just like you would with a putter. (See Crosby Three.) Play it high or low depending on side roll, faster or slower depending on up or down-slope. But also remember, since the club face isn't flat like a putter, you're going to get more overspin than with a putter. The ball will go further. You don't have to hit it hard to get it where you're going.

A Half Circle of Tees

First, place five golf tees in a half circle, three feet from the pin, around the back of the hole. That half circle is your target. Notice it's around the back of the pin, because the ball can't go in the hole if it stops in front of the pin. Once you get this close to the hole, your goal is sink the shot. Next, walk around the perimeter of the green, two to four feet into the fringe, dropping a batch of five or six balls every few feet around the green.

TEES AROUND HOLE

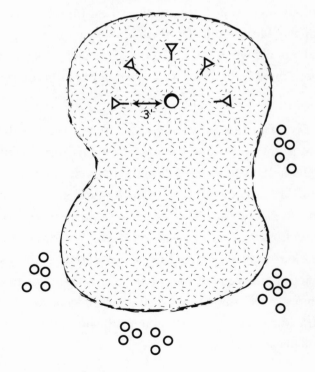

Starting with the first batch of balls, gauge the distance to the pin and read the green. Open your stance and play the ball off of your back toe. Angle your hands slightly toward your front knee, letting your weight move to your front foot, then grip the club near the bottom of the leather, with the club toe on the ground. Now draw the club back and release. What you're using here is really a putter stroke. Think about the clock from the pitching exercise. Take the club back less than seven o'clock. Swing through smoothly, like a well-stroked putt. You want the ball to land one-quarter of the way to the pin and run the remaining three-quarters of the way.

SIX-IRON HOP AND RUN

Watch the loft and roll of the ball. Did you give it enough to get it to the hole? Did you give it too much? Are you hitting the half-circle target? Too short or too long? Recalibrate your backswing to the correct clock position. Realign the shot to play the roll of the green. Now try the next one, and the next. Think putting, not hitting. Move to the next batch and repeat the routine until you've worked your way all the way around the green, adjusting the tee circle as you go.

Club 2—the eight-iron loft-and-roll. Step back to about four to ten feet off the green and walk around again, dropping batches of balls every few feet. When you add in the distance to the pin, say twenty or twenty-five feet, you should be twenty-four to thirty-five feet, or up to about twelve yards, from the hole, perfect eight-iron chipping range. You're going to get more loft, more carry, some backspin, and consequently less roll. So, where the ball lands should be closer to where it ends up.

Repeat the exercise as you did it with the six-iron, only now with the eight. Go to the first batch of balls and line up your shot. Use the same stance as you did with the six-iron, same weighting, grip, and ball position. Think of the shot as a strong putt or soft chip. Again, picture the clock and take the club back no farther than seven o'clock. You're very close to the hole and should need no more backswing than that. Now, take the club back and release. You want the ball to land one-third of the way to pin and run up the other two-thirds. Chip your way around the green, adjusting for roll, slope, and green speed.

EIGHT-IRON LOFT AND ROLL

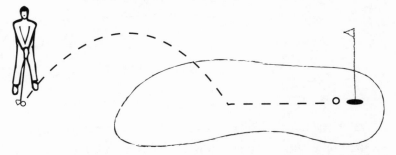

How close did you come to the cup? How many balls landed in the half circle of tees? Did any shots hit the pin? Did you sink any shots? Find the toughest spot and repeat the drill from there.

Club 3—the pitching wedge pop-and-stop. Once you get into a situation where the distance from the ball to the fringe is roughly equal to the distance from the fringe to the pin, you're ready to chip with your pitching wedge. In other words, if the ball is fifteen feet off the fringe and the pin is fifteen feet from the fringe, use the wedge. You're now too far to use your six- or eight-iron; you're going to get too much roll. If the pin is thirty feet from where your ball sits, your six-iron could take the ball twenty or thirty feet past the hole; your eight-iron, at best, will send the ball ten feet past.

You need the pitching wedge, but think of it as entirely different than the pitching wedge at forty to ninety yards out. You're chipping now. This is your "pop-and-stop" club. You want to lift the ball up and drop it down, half the distance in the air and then half in roll to the pin.

Once again, walk around the green and drop those batches of balls. Then go back and work on your pop-and-stop shots. You're going to open your stance a little more, open the face of the club a little farther, and play the ball back a bit more than with the eight iron. Think of the clock. Take the club back between seven and eight o'clock. Swing through easy. Work your way around the green, adjusting your backswing, ball position, and alignment.

WEDGE POP AND STOP

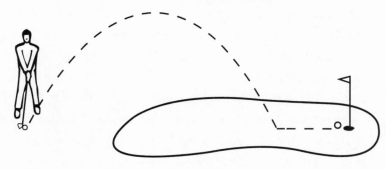

Use the green to help you. Play the undulations, the up and downward slopes. You don't want a lot of roll; you want control. You want to be inside the half circle of golf tees. The pin is your target, nothing less. You can aim for the fairway when you're on the tee. Aim for the green when you're in the fairway. But when you're this close, aim for the cup. The sooner you get there, the sooner you stop counting strokes.

Remember, chipping is all about "feel." The more you do this exercise, the more comfortable you will become in knowing which club to use in what situation. Does it call for a six or an eight? A soft six? A firmer eight? Do you need the wedge? More open-faced? Shorter backswing? Keep circling the green until you know the limits and range of each club in your Three-Club Bag.

Creativity, the Extra Club in Your Bag

You've got to be able to use the whole Three-Club Bag around the green—the six-iron, eight-iron, and wedge—whichever one works in a particular situation. Tiger was and is as creative as the situation demands. Who knows, after a while you may even try the shot Tiger does where he runs his ball up out of the rough with a three-wood. (On second thought, don't rush into this one.) The point is, don't pick a club automatically. Assess first, then decide. *Whatever the situation demands.*

If a shot demands more run than the eight-iron will get you but less than the six, there's always the seven. If it calls for more loft than an eight but less than a wedge, use the nine-iron.

You don't have to be in the sand to hit a sand wedge. Say the distance from the fringe to the pin is less than the distance from the fringe to the ball—the pin is ten feet from the fringe but your ball is fifteen feet from the edge of the green. You need a lot of loft and very little roll, or as much backspin as possible. The sand wedge will give you more than the pitching wedge. Open up the club face and you'll get the most. (But, for many of us, the sand wedge is a little tougher to hit. Use it if and when you're comfortable with it. Otherwise, hit the club that gives you confidence. That's a rule that applies from tee to green on all eighteen holes.)

Sometimes the best of the three clubs isn't any of them. Sometimes the best chip shot is a putt. Most people are more confident with a putter in their hands, especially those with handicaps over ten, but sometimes it even applies to pros. In a recent British Open, John Daly and others were putting from ten, twelve, or even fifteen feet off the green, because the conditions allowed them to do it. Just like the rest of us, pros want maximum control. Why pitch when you can putt? Remember, *whatever the situation demands.*

TECHNIQUE:
Play Par-3 Courses

Some people (what I call the golf snobs) say, "I'm not playing such-and-such course. It's not a real golf course; it's a par 3." No pun intended, but that's shortsighted. Playing a par-3 course could be the best practice your game ever gets.

When Tiger was a kid, he played a par-3 course in Long Beach called Hartwell. Most of the holes there are 120 yards or shorter, but that's not to say they're easy. You have to hit the ball on the green or very, very near it to make par. Tiger played this course all the time, nothing but par 3s. Around the time he was nine or ten years old, he won a club championship at Hartwell, that's how good he got at par 3s.

I like to have my teams play par-3 courses like Hartwell and another one called Bixby Village. If I know they can make threes and fours on par 3s consistently, I know they can score on a regulation course. Our goal is to get rid of the fours. What happens is, they're playing inside 100 to 120 yards but they're playing real situations, not just range shots. They're hitting a full eight-iron to an elevated green surrounded by bunkers. The ball lands on a downward slope, six feet into the fringe, eighteen feet from the pin, which is sitting beneath two mounds on a fresh-cut, fast green. In other words, they're literally playing the last hundred yards of what could be a par 4.

If you play a par-3 course well, just add one to two shots per hole to your score and you're playing a regulation course. If you can shoot par on a par-3 course, that's 54, plus, say, one shot per hole for sixteen par 4s, and two shots for two par 5s, that's 74, which I'm betting is better than your average score. If you shoot half pars and half bogeys on the par-3 course, that's still 63, plus one more on each par 4, and two more on each par 5, for a total of 83. Any way you figure it, if you get good at par 3s, you're going to lower your score.

When the golf snobs ask you how you got so good, tell them you played par-3 courses . . . like Tiger Woods.

LIKE ALL KIDS, TIGER PLAYED IN THE SAND

Playing out of sand traps is the worst nightmare of most golfers. It doesn't matter that we've all been told, over and over, that sand shots really aren't so difficult and our aversion to them is psychological. The nightmare feels real when your ball is buried up to its logo in hot sand, a lonely white speck on a beach as big as Big Sur, under the shadow of a bunker lip that looks like the overbite of a great white shark coming off a diet.

Let me be the first to agree that sand shots, in reality, aren't difficult. And let me disagree that our aversion to them is psychological. It couldn't be more logical. How can you get good at what you can't practice? The world is full of driving ranges and putting greens. But where is the nearest practice trap? Can you hit sand shots in your backyard? The most practice you get in traps is when you're playing a course and you're trying your best to avoid the sand.

The average golfer tries to learn how to hit out of a trap by watching a video. You can get very good at pushing the PLAY, PAUSE, and REWIND buttons and still not know if you're getting the hang of blasting the ball out of the bunker.

Tiger Woods was a good sand player from the moment I met him and probably for many years before that. How did he do it if there are so few places to practice? He found one. In his case, it was

Tiger with his coach and Jack Nicklaus.

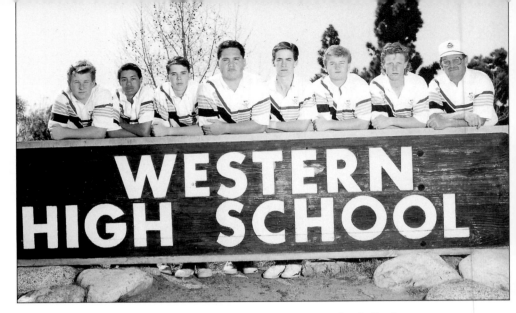

Western High School Varsity Golf Team, 1991—Tiger's freshman year. Left to right: Dustin Blood, Tiger Woods, Bryon Bell, Mike Kruse, Gary Holder, Craig Black, Mickey Conahan, Coach Crosby.

Scorecard

MARBELLA GOLF AND COUNTRY CLUB

Tee _____

Time _____ CIF-SCGA INDIVIDUAL CHAMPIONSHIP

COURSE RATINGS / SLOPE

Gentlemen's
- ☐ Tournament 72.2
- ☐ Championship ... 69.9
- ☐ Regular 67.6
- ☐ Forward 65.4

Ladies'
- ☐ Championship ....
- ☐ Regular.............
- ☐ Forward ....

HOLE	1	2	3	4	5	6	7	8	9	OUT		10	11	12	13	14	15	16	17	18	IN	Tot		
TOURNAMENT	406	463	315	206	490	393	153	466	434	3326		434	150	286	392	521	426	199	396	428	3232	6558		
CHAMPIONSHIP	366	404	302	186	475	360	143	430	415	3081		418	127	271	380	506	408	180	380	414	3084	6165		
REGULAR	352	389	292	165	460	332	132	392	393	2907		373	117	261	348	485	396	161	339	391	2871	5778		
FORWARD	307	338	271	142	449	305	122	345	360	2639		354	99	251	321	423	365	143	315	375	2646	5285		

TIGER WOODS AM ③ 4 4 5 ④ 4 3 4 5 36   4 3 4 4 ④ 4 4 4 4 35 71
+/- -1 -1 -1 +1 e e e e +1   e e e e -1 -1 e e

| PAR | 4 | 4 | 4 | 3 | 5 | 4 | 3 | 4 | 4 | 35 | | 4 | 3 | 4 | 4 | 5 | 4 | 3 | 4 | 4 | 35 | 70 | | |
| HANDICAP | 9 | 1 | 13 | 15 | 5 | 11 | 17 | 3 | 7 | | | 4 | 18 | 14 | 10 | 2 | 8 | 16 | 6 | 12 | | | | |

PM 4 4 4 3 ④ 5 3 4 4 35   ③ 3 5 4 ④ 3 3 4 ③ 32 67
+/- e e e e -1 e e e e   -1 e e +1 -2 -2 -2 -3

DATE 6/10/91   SCORER D Crosby   ATTEST _____

Tiger won the state championship in his freshman year. They played thirty-six holes in one day. In his second round in eight hours, Tiger made five birdies and shot 67!

HOLE	1	2	3	4	5	6	7	8	9	OUT
Championship Tees	326	372	385	259	300	429	227	455	172	2925
Regular Tees	305	357	372	251	293	411	205	440	150	2784
Handicap	9	7	3	17	15	1	5	13	11	
Men's Par	4	4	4	4	4	4	3	5	3	35
WOODS	4	5	4	2	3	3	4	4	2	31
Pullium	4	4	5	4	4	4	5	5	6	39

	10	11	12	13	14	15	16	17	18	IN	TOTAL			
	468	107	359	131	348	369	198	614	507	3101	6026	SCGA Slope 107 ☐		
	457	100	341	119	337	348	168	607	495	2972	5756	SCGA Slope 103 ☐		
	14	18	4	16	12	8	10	2	6					
	5	3	4	3	4	4	3	5	5	36	71	HDC	NET	ADJ

HOLE	1	2	3	4	5	6	7	8	9	OUT
Kruse	4	5	6	5	3	4	3	5	4	39
Beliveau	7	7	5	7	6	7	5	7	5	56
Ladies' Par	4	4	4	4	4	4	3	5	3	35
Handicap	9	7	1	15	11	3	13	5	17	
LADIES' TEES	284	328	359	244	277	368	162	426	125	2573

	10	11	12	13	14	15	16	17	18	IN	TOTAL		
Ladies' Par	5	3	4	3				6	5	37	72		
Handicap	2	16	8	18	12	10	14	4	6				
	440	92	322	100	289	329	163	600	470	2805	5378	Course Slope 107 ☐	

H.G. "Dad" Miller Golf Course, 430 N. Gilbert St., Anaheim, CA

Date: Scorer: Attest:

PGA GOLF PROFESSIONAL—BOB JOHNS

As a sophomore, Tiger put together five birdies for a 31 against Magnolia High School. Note, Tiger signed this card.

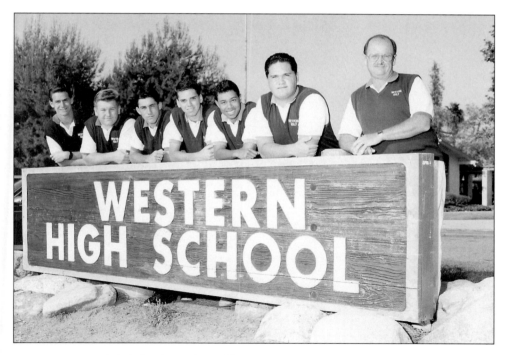

Western High School Varsity Golf Team, 1992. Left to right: Gary Holder, Dustin Blood, Jeff Anderson, Bryon Bell, Tiger Woods, Mike Kruse, Coach Crosby.

CANYON COUNTRY CLUB — PALM SPRINGS, CA

HOLE	1	2	3	4	5	6	7	8	9	OUT		10	11	12	13	14	15	16	17	18	IN	TOT	HCP
CHAMPIONSHIP	378	392	434	192	441	547	164	389	395	3332		493	417	428	556	201	338	192	368	498	3491	6823	
REGULAR	352	371	411	170	421	522	152	373	372	3144		470	388	407	535	173	320	153	349	480	3275	6419	
HANDICAP - Men	13	5	3	15	1	9	17	11	7			12	4	2	8	16	18	14	6	10			
TIGER WOODS	4	4	4	3	4	5	4	4	4	36	COURSE RATING	5	4	4	(4)	3	(3)	3	(3)	(3)	32	68	
											Champion 72.9												
CIF- SS CHAMPIONSHIP											Regular 70.3												
PAR - Men & Ladies	4	4	4	3	4	5	3	4	4	35		5	4	4	5	3	4	3	4	5	37	72	
											Ladies 72.2												
HANDICAP - Ladies	7	9	3	15	1	11	17	13	5			12	4	2	10	16	14	18	8	6			
LADIES YDS.	328	329	381	123	389	464	103	343	332	2792		450	354	381	478	147	301	105	320	455	2991	5783	

Tiger won the Southern Section California Interscholastic Federation Championship in 1991 with a 68. He started on hole 10 and shot a five-under-par 32. Half of the field started on hole number one.

CONTESTANT **TIGER WOODS**   SCHOOL **WESTERN HS**

DATE **MAY 24, 1993**   1993   COACH **DON CROSBY**

TEE **# 10**   TIME **9 28**   CIF SOUTHERN SECTION INDIVIDUAL CHAMPIONSHIPS

HOLES	1	2	3	4	5	6	7	8	9	OUT		10	11	12	13	14	15	16	17	18	OUT	TOTAL
Yards	378	392	434	192	441	547	164	389	395	3332		493	417	428	556	201	338	192	368	498	3491	6823
Par	4	4	4	3	4	5	3	4	4	35		5	4	4	5	3	4	3	4	5	37	72
	4	4	(3)	3	4	5	3	4	(3)	33		5	(3)	(3)	5	3	(3)	3	5	5	35	68

CONTESTANT'S SIGNATURE   *CHIPED SAND SAVE*

MARKER'S SIGNATURE

HOLES	1	2	3	4	5	6	7	8	9	OUT		10	11	12	13	14	15	16	17	18	IN	TOTAL
MY SCORE																						

Tiger swept the Southern Section California Interscholastic Federation Championship in 1993 with a four-under-par 68.

Tiger at the star-studded headtable with Dial's female athlete/scholar winner, All-American volleyball player Kristin Fokhl. Coincidentally, both Tiger and Kristen went to Stanford.

La Cumbre Golf & Country Club
4015 Via Laguna   Santa Barbara, CA 93110
Pro Shop (805) 682-3131   Office (805) 687-2421

Course Designers
William Bell (1928)
William Bell, Jr. (1957)

PLAYER

Scorer _____
Attest _____
Date _____

*13 Island Green
Blue: 195 Yards
White: 164 Yards
Gold: 112 Yards
Red: 99 Yards

RATINGS: COURSE · SLOPE · TP PLAYED

		1	2	3	4	5	6	7	8	9	Out		10	11	12	13	14	15	16	17	18	In	Tot	Rating	Slope	TP
Blue	Yardage	415	358	393	364	154	522	156	348	472	3182		495	168	529	215	413	378	411	156	405	3170	6352	70.8	128	□
White	Yardage	391	350	373	339	146	513	148	342	464	3066		483	148	479	190	381	363	401	144	385	2974	6040	69.1	120	□
Men's	Handicap	7	3	9	11	15	1	17	13	5			14	16	2	10	4	12	6	18	8					
Men's	Par	4	4	4	4	3	5	3	4	5	36		5	3	5	3	4	4	4	3	4	35	71			
TIGER WOODS		(3)	4	4	4	3	7	(2)	4	5	36		(4)	3	5	(2)	(3)	(3)	4	(2)	4	30	66			
		1	2	2	2	2	2	1	2	2	16		1	1	2	1	1	1	2	1	1	11				
							8				8											7				

Assoc#	HOLE	1	2	3	4	5	6	7	8	9	Out		10	11	12	13	14	15	16	17	18	In	Tot	Hcp	Net	Adj
Women's	Par	4	4	4	4	3	5	3	4	5	36		5	3	5	3	4	4	5	3	4	36	72			
Women's	Handicap	7	11	5	9	15	1	17	13	3			4	16	2	14	12	10	8	18	6					
Red	Yardage	389	316	363	321	138	503	126	324	443	2923		453	137	452	134	356	336	406	132	372	2778	5701	73.0	128	□

In Tiger's senior year, he won the CIF Southern Section Championship once more, this time with a 66. He went five under on the back nine for a 30!

Western High School Varsity Golf Team, 1993. Left to right: Greg Senglaub, Matt Sergott, Joe Hallada, David Dawson, Bryon Bell, Tiger Woods, Mike Hansen, Coach Crosby.

HOLE	1	2	3	4	5	6	7	8	9	OUT
CHAMPIONSHIP	326	372	385	259	300	429	227	455	172	2925
REGULAR	305	357	372	251	293	411	205	440	150	2784
HANDICAP	9	7	3	17	15	1	5	13	11	
PAR	4	4	4	4	4	4	3	5	3	35
WOODS										
BELL										
Harper										
Waldrop										
PAR	4	4	4	4	4	4	3	5	3	35
HANDICAP	9	7	1	15	11	3	13	5	17	
LADIES'	284	328	359	244	277	368	162	426	125	2573

H.G. "Dad" Miller Golf Course, 430 N. Gilbert St., Anaheim, CA
Bob Johns, PGA Golf Professional

HOLE	10	11	12	13	14	15	16	17	18	IN	TOT	Course Rating	SCGA Slope
CHAMPIONSHIP	468	107	359	131	348	369	193	614	507	3096	6021	68.0	108
REGULAR	457	100	341	119	337	348	168	607	495	2972	5756	66.4	105
HANDICAP	14	18	4	16	12	8	10	2	6				
PAR	5	3	4	3	4	4	3	5	5	36	71	HCP	NET	ADJ
PAR	4	3	4	3	4	4	3	6	5	37	72		
HANDICAP	2	16	8	18	12	10	14	4	6			Course Rating	SCGA Slope
LADIES'	440	92	322	100	289	329	147	600	470	2789	5362	70.0	107

DATE   SCORER   ATTEST

In a nine-hole match against Savanna High School, Tiger shot a five-under-par 30!

Coach Crosby with 1994 seniors. Left to right: Amber Reaume, Tiger Woods, John Nichols, and Bryon Bell.

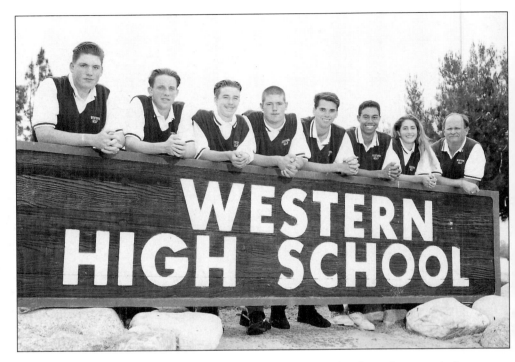

Western High School Varsity Golf Team, 1994—Tiger's senior year. Left to right: Ben Snyder, Joe Hallada, David Dawson, Vince Branstetter, Bryon Bell, Tiger Woods, Amber Reaume, Coach Crosby.

the navy base in Los Alamitos. They actually had a trap at the far end of the practice range. He could go there and hit sand shots all day. He could experiment. He could make mistakes that didn't cost him a shot on his scorecard. So, even when he was little, while his dad was hitting off the tee, Tiger was hitting out of the sand. He got as familiar with hitting sand wedges as the rest of us are with hitting drives (the one shot we probably practice too much). He never had a psychological aversion to sand shots because he practiced them until they were routine.

LESSON:
To Get Out of the Sand,
You Have to Get into the Sand

Here's the first and most important lesson in hitting sand shots. Do what you'd never do when you're playing a round of golf. Get in a sand trap on purpose. Find a range that has a practice trap, even if you have to drive a long way to get there. Or go out to a course very early or very late, find an empty hole with a big, ugly, mean trap, and drop a bag of balls in the sand. When you're playing and there's no one behind you, even if your ball didn't go in the trap, drop two or three in there and hit them out. Look for every opportunity to hit sand shots when they don't count, so you'll be better when they do.

To most players, the idea of purposely going looking for sand is like asking Evander Holyfield to hit you so you can get used to it. But think of it as learning to duck when he swings.

How to Get Out of a Trap in
One Shot Every Time

Okay, once you've found your practice trap, work on these five trap tricks.

1. Lighten up, don't tighten up. Most people tend to grip hard when they get in the sand. The tension they feel becomes a choke hold on the club. The result is, when you swing the club, you hit hard and dig too deep. You want to do the opposite. Ease up on your grip and just take a shallow divot.

GRIP PRESSURE

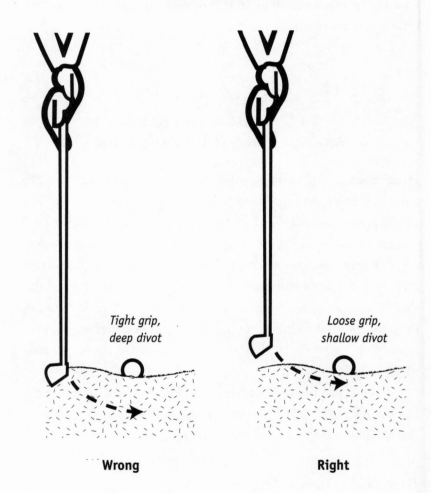

Tight grip, deep divot

Loose grip, shallow divot

Wrong

Right

2. Use the fast break. When you go into your backswing, you should break your wrists quickly. You know that nice, smooth arc with the long, low takeaway you try so hard to achieve on the practice range and in the fairway? Forget it in the trap. In the sand, you take the club back, break your wrists early, creating more of a U-shaped swing than a half circle or arc swing. You bring the club back down and follow through just as quickly. That literally brings the ball out of the sand sooner, sends it up and out, but not too far, only as far as the green.

U-SHAPED SWING

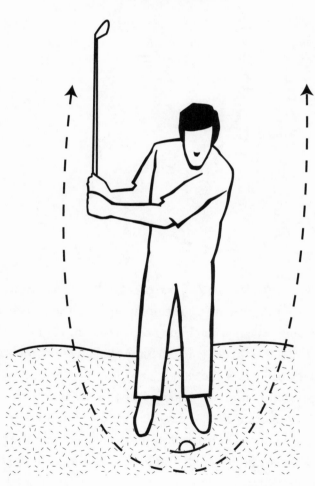

3. Open wide. When you're in the sand, you want your club face open and you want your stance open. Not just open as in an off-the-green chip shot. Really open. I try to get my players to point their back foot away from the pin at a 45-degree angle with their front foot not parallel to the back one, but pulled back several inches (see diagram). But the club face is still aimed right at the pin, or perpendicular to it. The result is to open the swing up and make it even more upright or U-shaped for maximum lift.

OPEN CLUB FACE IN SAND

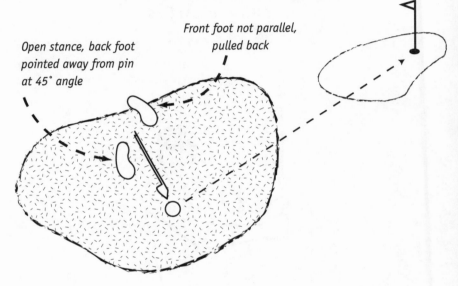

Open stance, back foot pointed away from pin at 45° angle

Front foot not parallel, pulled back

4. Aim carefully and miss the ball. Normally when you address the ball, you put your club up pretty close to its back side. But I tell my players when hitting out of the sand not to look at the ball, because they're not going to hit the ball. Instead, look at a spot behind the ball where the club is going to enter the sand. What you need to decide before you swing is how far behind the ball you want the club to enter the sand—anywhere from an inch to an inch and a half behind the ball. That way, you can't skull or top the ball, driving it further into the trap. You hit the sand behind the ball and then let the swing carry the sand and the ball up and onto the green.

HITTING BEHIND BALL IN SAND

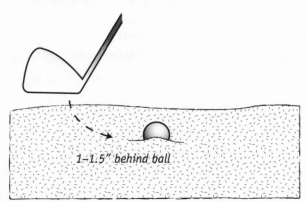

1–1.5" behind ball

5. Play nice. Throw sand. The biggest mistake I see people make in traps is that they hit the sand and stop. If you don't throw some sand on the green, the ball is not going to get out of the trap. The only way to throw sand is for your follow-through to be equal to your backswing. If you take your club away shoulder high, you want to follow through shoulder high. Many players fear that following through means hitting the ball too hard and too far, so they try to punch it out. More times than not, you'll just punch it further into the sand. After all, sand is porous. Like all good golf shots, you have to swing through to get the ball to go where you want.

FOLLOW-THROUGH AND SAND-THROW

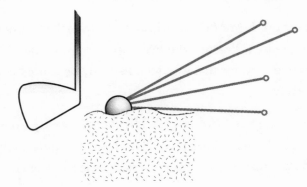

TECHNIQUE:
Your Two-by-Four Wood

This is an adaptation of a drill my team and I saw at the Jim McClean School of Golf at PGA West in Palm Springs. I modify it a little from the way they taught it, but the idea is pretty much the same.

Get a twenty-four-inch two-by-four. Go to that practice trap you've found. Take along a piece of wood, a two-by-four, about twenty-four inches long. You could probably use something else about that size, anything that's pretty solid and that you don't mind damaging a little. (I've thought about an old hardcover book, but I'm reluctant to tell my players for fear they'll use a schoolbook.)

Bury the board. Walk into the trap and line yourself up as if you're going to hit a shot toward the pin. Take the two-by-four and lay it down in front of your feet, parallel to your line at the hole. Now bury the board so it has about an inch of sand on top of it. Then, with your wedge, scoop a small mound of sand on top of the buried board, in a pile about an inch deep and four inches around.

Tee it up on sand. What you're going to do is hit the ball from that little mound- of-sand tee. With a board under the ball, you feel safe in hitting deep enough because you know the board will stop you. At the same time, that nice hard board prevents you from hitting too deep. It's almost like hitting off a practice-range mat.

Practice with the board. Hit one. Then make another sand tee and hit another. Practice the five trap tricks with each shot. After you hit twenty shots that way, you'll already be a more comfortable sand player.

Practice without the board. Hit another twenty from the same spot but without the board. You'll find you're hitting them the same way. What's happening is, you're visualizing a bottom under the

sand so you don't go too shallow or too deep. That's your groove
for sand shots.

BOARD IN SAND

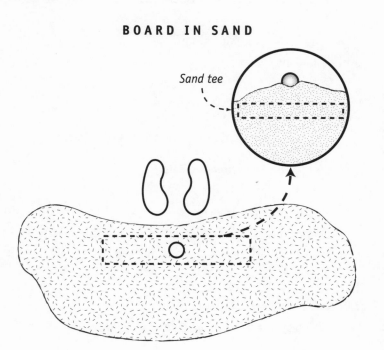

Sand tee

Of course, you'll adjust your backswing and the openness of
the club face, depending on the distance you need. Just keep practicing the five trap tricks, picture that bottom under the sand, and
what all those experts have been saying will finally be true. Sand
trap shots really aren't very difficult.

Crosby's Quick Refresher
CROSBY TWO—SHORT GAME

Routine removes anxiety.

LESSON: Pitching

The Pitching Clock—a dozen shots at each "hour"—7, 8, 9,
10, and 11 o'clock.

continued on page 60

continued from page 59

- Reset your clock—check and adjust distance at each "hour" mark.
- Fine tune your chip shots:
  - low into wind
  - lob for loft

GAME: *Field Goal Golf*

- Pitch over the goalposts from closest distance.

TECHNIQUE: *The Three-Club Bag*

- Six-iron—hop-and-run.
- Eight-iron—loft-and-roll.
- Wedge—pop-and-stop.
- Creativity—the extra club in your bag (know what to use, where).

TECHNIQUE: *Play Par-3 Courses*

- Like last one hundred yards of par 4s or 5s.

LESSON: *Sand*

> **To get out of the sand, you have to get in.**
> **Find a practice trap.**

- Lighten up, don't tighten up on your grip.
- Use fast break—break your wrists in backswing.
- Open wide—club face.
- Miss the ball—hit behind it.
- Throw sand—onto the green with ball.

TECHNIQUE: *Your Two-by-Four Wood*

- Bury block under sand to learn to hit deep, not too deep.

CROSBY THREE

Putting.
The little matter of getting
the ball in the hole.

INSIGHT:
In-Betweeners, or, Why Otherwise Good Golfers Are Often Mediocre Putters

By now, you should know the answer. It's my favorite word: practice. I know what you're thinking. "Hold on, Coach, I do practice my putting. I go out to the putting green before every round, or while I'm waiting for the rest of my foursome, or after I've just finished, any time I have a spare moment." Great. But exactly how do you practice?

Chances are you go out to the putting green, drop a few balls down by one of the holes, and putt to the next hole, one hole at a time, from hole to hole. The holes are usually twenty-five or thirty feet apart. You rarely make one, so then you knock the one- or two-footers you've left yourself into the hole. You get pretty good at straight, flat twenty-five to thirty-footers and one-foot gimmes. How often does that situation occur on the golf course? Three, maybe four times. What about all the ten-footers, three-footers, and five-footers? What about the downhill racers or sidehill snakes? The bumps and rolls? Those are the putts that can make or break a round of golf, the ones that can mean the difference between a 96 and breaking 90, shooting 85 or being in the 70s. But golfers rarely practice them. They just get good at lagging the ball up twenty-five feet.

You have to practice what really happens, what I call the "in-betweeners," the three-to-six-footers. You have to gain confidence with them. You have to feel like you're going to hit them in, not like you might hit them in. Did you ever notice that when you stand over a twenty-two-foot putt you're not as nervous as when you stand over a five-foot putt? That's because nobody (including you) expects you to make the long one. On the other hand, the short one is short enough that you should make it but just long enough for things to go wrong. I'm going to give you some drills that will leave you with the confidence to know an in-betweener is almost a sure thing.

LESSON:
There's Only One Way to Putt: Straight

There are only two kinds of putts: (1) straight and (2) not straight. Most people will say there are all kinds, long and short, fast and slow, breaking left and right, uphill and downhill. But they're all just variations on straight and not straight.

No matter what kind of putt you face—straight or not straight—you still always want to hit the ball straight. (Leave it to the ground to make it go not straight.) Of course, it seems like it ought to be easy to putt the ball straight, but there are any number of ways to unintentionally make it go left, right, or even a little of both.

To Putt Straight, You Have to Putt Smooth

Putting is like Goldilocks and the Three Bears. Your stroke and your porridge have to be just right. If you're too hot, your ball will go past the hole, and if you're too cold, you'll leave the ball way short of the hole. If you use a jerky back swing and a hurry-up or slow-down follow-through, there's no telling where the ball will go. I have two simple techniques I use to teach players a smooth, steady stroke.

TECHNIQUE:
Underhand Lob

Putting is about hand speed. What I do is take my players about fifteen feet from the hole and give them each two golf balls. I tell them to lob the balls, underhand, toward the cup. Because many of us grow up knowing how to throw, how much exertion it takes to get a ball from here to there and not beyond, most people will lob the ball pretty close to the hole. It's only when we put a stick in our hands that we lose that feel.

I have the players do that lob several times. Then I explain that the motion of lobbing—swinging back, then through, easily and gently—is a putting motion. Try it and you'll see, it doesn't take much of a toss to get the ball to the hole. Keep doing it until you feel comfortable lagging the ball up to the hole.

Then pick up your putter but think "underhand lob." Fix that image in your mind as you stroke the putter. Even when you take your practice putts before the real one, imagine that lob motion in your mind. Then take your nice, easy stroke. You'll be amazed how thinking "lob" will translate to putting smooth.

TECHNIQUE:
Look at the Hole, Not the Ball

I know, I know. In every sport, they tell you to keep your eye on the ball. I say it in golf. "When you're on the tee, look at the ball, not where it's going." When you're in the fairway, rough, or sand, you should keep your eyes riveted on the ball. Even when you're putting, not just practicing, you should look at the ball.

But when you are practicing and you want to imbed a smooth stroke in your mind, look at the hole, not the ball. That way, you're looking at how far away your target sits, thinking what it takes to get the ball there. It makes you "see" your stroke in your mind but not concentrate on the point of impact with the ball. It makes you act by feel, not force. Notice how close you can get the ball by only looking at the hole. There are even a few pros who now putt for the money that way.

To Putt the Ball Straight,
You Have to Putt the Putter Straight

Once you master a smooth stroke, the only ways to go wrong are variations on not taking the putter back straight or following through straight. If you pull the putter back left, you'll hit the ball to the right. If you pull it back right, the ball will go left. If you punch it, the ball will pop off the club and could go either way. If you waggle on the backswing, you'll waggle when you strike the ball and it'll waggle its way across the green.

There's only one way to make the ball go straight. Hit it straight. Back straight and through straight. Practice on the three- to six-foot shadows (as described below), putting the ball straight at the hole, over and over. Hit twelve in a row. Try to make the ball never leave the shadow line. Walk to another shadow in a flat area. Hit twelve more. Make that three- to six-foot distance as familiar as a one-footer. As the sun moves, it will make the shadows longer or shorter but never beyond the distances you'll face most often on the course. Use the Crosby Really Cheap and Chalkless Chalk Line. The sun is there for all of us to use.

TECHNIQUE:
Crosby's Really Cheap and Chalkless Chalk Line

The way many pros teach straight-line putting is the chalk line method. They take a chalk line, that is, a piece of string coated in chalk, find a flat section of the green, stick one end of the string down at a point, say, four to six feet from the hole, then walk to the hole, hold the other end of the string at the lip of the cup, snap the string, and leave a straight line of chalk from the starting point all the way to the hole. Then they drop a few balls at the starting point and have you practice putting the ball so it follows the chalk all the way into the cup.

The Crosby's Really Cheap and Chalkless Chalk Line requires no purchase of equipment, leaves no dusty chalk on your hands, and can't be mistakenly left at home. All you need is the sun. Go to the putting green in late afternoon. The flags on the green, which are three or four feet tall, will cast a narrow shaft of shadow about three to six feet long, depending on time of day. Thanks to physics, that shadow will always be a straight line.

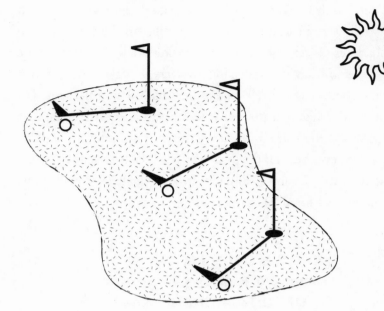

Now, you just find one of those shadows that's cast across a flat section of the green and you have an instant chalk line, free. Lay a ball down right on the line, so the shadow cuts your ball in half. What you want to do is stroke the ball so it hugs that shadow all the way up to and into the cup.

GAME:
Worst of Both

Improve your short putts

You've heard of golf tournaments called "best balls" where everyone hits the first shot and then the team takes the best resulting shot and hits from there for their second shot, then hits the best of the second ones for the third shot, and so on. Well, this is the opposite.

In this game or drill, you start a little farther from the hole than with the chalk line exercise. You can even go from hole to hole, or up to twenty-five feet. Putt two balls toward the hole. Let's say one ends up three inches from the hole. Nice putt. But the other is a foot and half short. Too bad. Don't tap in the close one. Take the "worst of both" and putt both from there. Move the three-incher next to the one a foot and a half away. Now putt both balls from that spot. You don't need much practice with tap-ins, but you need all you can get with one- and two-footers.

WORST OF BOTH PUTTING GAME

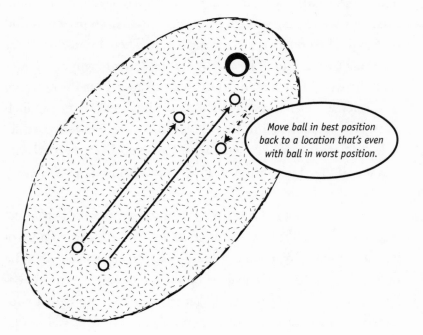

Move ball in best position back to a location that's even with ball in worst position.

Do that all the way around the putting green. Putt two first shots. One you leave two feet shy of the hole but the other is hanging on the lip of the cup. Great. But don't wait for a breeze to blow it in. Move it all the way back to the two-foot spot and putt both from there. The great thing about this drill is, good is good and bad is good. A good putt is a good putt and a bad putt is good practice.

CROSBY THREE—PUTTING. THE LITTLE MATTER OF GETTING THE BALL IN THE HOLE

TIGER'S GAME:
Pullback

Where a one-inch putt can be three feet

When Tiger was in high school, he invented this game to make it fun to practice middle-range putts. He called it the Pullback Game. Here's how it works:

He'd get one of the other guys on the team to go head-to-head in a round on the putting green, playing for pennies or a soda, anything to add to the game. It wasn't smart to play against him in Pullback, but even losing was good for your game. Both players would putt to the first hole on the putting green. Then, no matter where your ball landed, you'd have to pull it back the length of a putter shaft (between thirty and thirty-six inches) away from the hole. So, if you were an inch away, you could now be three feet and an inch away. If you happened to hit it badly and were two feet past the hole, now you were looking at a five-foot putt. Every second shot was a middle-range putt. And if you didn't sink it, so was every third putt, and every fourth.

If you weren't good at three-to-six-footers, you were in trouble. Needless to say, Tiger was very good at them. He earned a lot of free sodas that way. He never got a case of nerves even when he pulled the ball back. He thrived on the competition. Why? Crosby's favorite reason: practice. Tiger practiced the putts that happened on the course, the middle-range putts, so they were more routine to him than to the other guy.

The putting moral is, why just get good at the twenty-five-footers you'll face on maybe three holes when you can get good at the three-to-six-footers you're going to face on the other fifteen holes? Which one will take your score down faster?

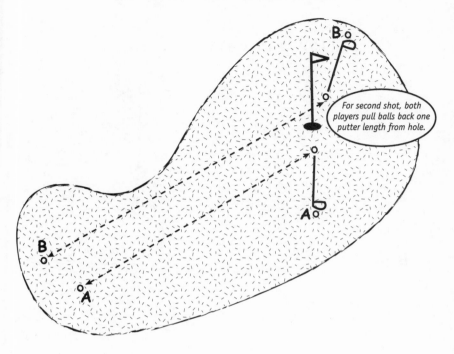

For second shot, both players pull balls back one putter length from hole.

GAME:
Too Bad

A Variation on Pullback

One of the things we all learned from Tiger is it's better to putt the ball past the hole than to leave it short. The ball simply cannot go into the hole unless it gets to the hole. Sounds obvious, but an awful lot of people keep putting the ball a little closer and a little closer. They attempt to sneak up on the hole instead of just trying to sink the ball in it.

Be an aggressive putter. Give yourself a chance to make a birdie or a par. In order to drive that point home, we invented a variation on the Pullback Game that I call Too Bad, as in, "too bad you putted short instead of long." Too Bad works just like the Pullback Game except that if you putt the ball up to or past the hole, you play it where it lies. If you putt the ball short of the hole, then you have to take it back another club length and putt from there.

TOO-BAD PUTTING GAME

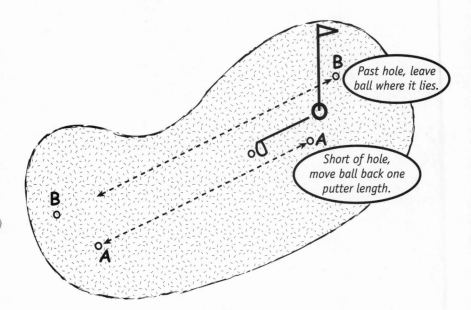

Think about it. If you're playing against me and I hit the ball a foot past the hole, I putt from there. If you leave yours six inches short, you play it from a club length plus six inches back, or about three feet. I have a tap-in and you have a real putt. We play nine holes and keep score. It doesn't take many rounds of Too Bad to teach you to putt aggressively. Sneaking up only costs you.

The idea is, you want to stroke the ball not just up to the hole, but into it. That means you're putting for the middle of the cup. Don't just hope it'll keel over and fall in from the front lip like an actor doing a bad death scene. Go for the hole, nothing less. You might make the putt and you might not. But if you leave it short, you definitely won't make it. You just give yourself an unnecessary penalty, and that's . . . too bad.

A great place to watch aggressive putting is the Nike Tour. These young players are doing everything they can to move up to the PGA Tour. They're not about to miss finishing in the money just because they left a four-footer short of the hole. Watch Tiger and you'll see how often he actually bangs the ball into the back of the cup. There's no mistake about his stroke.

Chip short. Putt long.

There is one implication of aggressive putting that isn't so aggressive. Chipping. You can be a lot bolder with an uphill putt than a downhill putt. (Downhill putts are powered by gravity, no matter how softly you hit them.) So, when you chip, you want to leave the ball below the hole, not above it. That way, when you putt you can really give the ball a firm, meaningful stroke, right at the hole.

IDEAL:
Straight and Smooth, Together

Combing these two elements is how you putt the ball in the hole with the minimum number of shots. Your stroke is smooth and steady. Your motion is straight back and straight through. You think "lob," you see the hole, and then you putt. The result: the right pace. The reward: fewer putts.

TECHNIQUE:
The Trough

The biggest mistake players make is taking the putter back too far before stroking the ball. Too many players bring the club back a foot or more when they're hitting a four-foot putt. That means you have to decelerate, or slow the putter way down, as it gets near the ball. (Otherwise you'll hit it another four feet past the hole.) The result is a jerky stroke. First fast—then stop—then slow.

What you want is a pendulum—same speed back as forward. The club is actually accelerating as it goes through the ball. On a four-foot putt, all you need is a few inches of backswing and the same in forward stroke.

If you want to make sure you take the club back smoothly, in a straight line, but not too far back, build a trough that prevents mistakes. Here's how you do it. (Needless to say, you don't have to buy anything.) Just take two of your other clubs and lay them down on the putting green two feet from the hole, heads away from the hole, shafts parallel to each other, about eight inches apart, with each club head pointed in toward the other. You've just formed a trough that leads right to the hole.

Figuring the average putter head at about six inches wide, the trough leaves you an inch from the toe and an inch from the heel of the putter head. Now place a ball down about six inches in from where the trough club heads come together. You're going to putt that ball into the hole. It's pretty obvious that you can't take the putter back more than six inches before you hit one of those club heads. If you take it back too far, you'll hear the loud clunk of club heads colliding. You have almost no choice but to take it back a short distance and accelerate a little on the follow-through. If you take the club back to one side or the other, you'll hit it off left or right. If you take the club straight back and come straight through, you'll hit the ball straight in the hole. The trough creates parallels to give you the line to the hole and a backstop to prevent overswinging. You're practicing "pace," or a smooth stroke, back and forth, a steady feel for putting the ball in the hole. More about pace in a moment.

After hitting several putts at one distance, move the trough back another foot from the hole. Place the ball down an additional inch away from the club heads to give yourself a bit more room to take your putter back. One inch more is about all you'll need.

Experiment with putting distances and backswing distances. Remember, it's better to have a small backswing and accelerate a little coming through the ball than to have too big a backswing and have to slow down coming through.

TWO-CLUB TROUGH

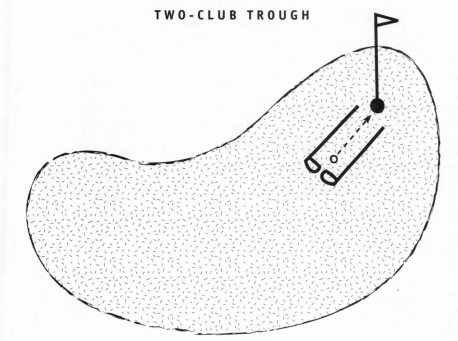

PACE TECHNIQUE:
Heel-against-Flagstick

Pace is a form of rhythm, almost like a metronome. If you take the putter straight back four inches, you want to come through four inches or more. You don't want to take it back six inches and then have to apply the brakes on the way forward. The way pace is achieved is by the action of your hands moving the club head back and forth. That's why I do this little demonstration with my players. I tell them to put the ball

(continued on page 74)

(continued from page 73)

in one hand, bend down toward the hole, and roll the ball to the hole. Usually, they get it pretty close. For most of us, our hands translate what our mind wants pretty accurately. But when I tell them to putt the ball from the same spot, invariably the putt isn't as close as the roll. You have to practice getting your hands to translate your thoughts to the club. You have to practice pace.

Tiger had a great little device for doing that—The Heel-against-Flagstick Technique. When it was someone else's turn to putt, he'd go over to where the flag pole was lying on the green and put his ball down near the it. With the heel of his putter against the pole, he'd try to stroke the ball so the club heel dragged right along the edge of the pole.

PUTTER HEEL
AGAINST FLAGSTICK

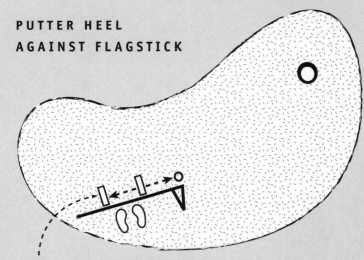

Stroke putter with heel against flagstick.

He took these little strokes, over and over, always with the heel of the putter kissing the pole. It made him stroke absolutely straight and made the ball go exactly parallel to the pole. Most of us could roll the ball parallel to the pole. Tiger was training his hands to get the club to do it just as well.

Crosby's Quick Refresher
CROSBY THREE—PUTTING

> **Putting Practice is NOT twenty-five-footers
> and one-foot gimmes.
> Putting Practice SHOULD BE in-betweeners—
> three-to-six-footers.**

LESSON: There's only one way to putt: Straight.
To putt straight, you have to putt smooth.

TECHNIQUE: The underhand lob
- Roll the ball toward the cup.

TECHNIQUE: Look at the hole, not the ball
To putt the ball straight, you have to putt the putter straight.

TECHNIQUE: The chalkless chalk line—pin shadows
- Putt along the shadows of the pins on the putting green.

GAME: Worst of Both
- Putt two balls, putt second shot from worse
  position of two.

TIGER'S GAME: Pullback
- Pull first putt back one putter length away from hole.

GAME: Too Bad
- Putt ball past hole or else move it back one putter
  length away from hole.

> **Chip short, putt long.**
> If your ball is off the green, below the hole, chip short
> of the hole to leave yourself with an uphill putt so you
> can still putt aggressively.

(continued on page 76)

(continued from page 75)

IDEAL: *Straight and smooth, together*

TECHNIQUE: *Trough Drill*

- Lay two clubs parallel on green to create trough to hole. Practice smooth stroke plus straight stroke. Result— pace and fewer putts.

PACE TECHNIQUE—*Heel-against-Flagstick*

- Lay flagstick down on green, rest heel of putter against flag, practice stroke that keeps heel touching stick.

CROSBY FOUR

Course management.
Getting smarter
than the golf course.

INSIGHT:
The Only Constant on the Golf Course
Is the Golf Course

There's only one constant in the game of golf. Golfers are human, so the constant sure isn't me or you. Some days you hit straighter or longer or more accurately than other days. Some days your putter is hot and some days ice cold. You fiddle with your grip, your stance, your weight, and your swing. You try new clubs, a new glove, and the latest tips from guys like me. One day you're on and the next day you're off. Plus, you tend to rise or fall to the level of your opponents or partners. No, the constant isn't us.

Nothing is more unpredictable than weather, so you know that's not the constant. It could be windy or still. If it's humid, the ball will hang in the air. If it's dry, the ball is going to fly. Bright sun may make you squint. Fresh rain can cut the roll of the ball.

The only constant on the golf course is the golf course itself. Oh sure, the grass may be longer or shorter. The pins get moved from time to time, as do the tees. But for the most part, the course stays the same. A par 72 tends to stay a par 72. A dogleg left on a Tuesday in April is a dogleg left on a Friday in August. That short par-3 over the pond on the front nine doesn't suddenly hop across the course and end up a long par-4 through the woods on the back side. The trees don't move. The traps rarely get bigger. (It just seems like they open wider when they see your ball coming.) The bunkers and water stay in the same places. And out-of-bounds is out-of-bounds is out-of-bounds.

But most golfers don't learn about the course before they play it. And once they do play a course, they don't benefit from the knowledge they've gained. Instead, if you're like most golfers, you just step up to the tee, look down the fairway, and swing. You don't plan each shot; you just hit it. You don't figure out what you're going to do next, only what you're doing right now, one shot at a time, all the way to the green and into the hole.

Say you're playing a par-4 and you hit your tee shot 220 yards down the left side, all the way to the clump of bushes at the dogleg. Wow, you hit a killer tee shot! But when you get to your ball, you see that the bushes block your line to the green so you have to take out your seven-iron and pop the ball over the bushes, back into the fairway, before you can get a clear shot again. Of course, the bushes were there before you teed off. You could have planned to hit a tee shot that was a little short and to the right of the bushes, leaving you a wide-open four-iron to the green, with a shot saved. But you would have had to *plan* it in advance. You have to manage the course instead of letting it manage you.

You can save yourself two shots a round, maybe more, just by good course management, by knowing the golf course you're playing. Think about it. Two free shots, there for the saving. Why would anyone pass them up?

TIGER, BEFORE COURSE MANAGEMENT

In Tiger's freshman year, our team had a match in Long Beach at a course called Recreation Park. Whenever we have an away match, we have a lunch meeting before we play. So, that day, all the kids stopped by office with their lunches. I handed them each a sheet of paper with a little map I'd drawn of the course. It wasn't a work of art, but it showed them which holes doglegged, where the major hazards were, how long the holes were, and other key information. Then we talked about how to play each one, which, of course, was different for each of our players.

I remember distinctly that I pointed out to them that the very first hole at Recreation was a fairly short par-4, only about 310 yards with a little dogleg to the right. I said, "Some of you guys can't hit a driver on this hole. It's too short. Think about a three-wood or long iron." Then we went on to the next hole and so on, right through the entire nine. I looked up and saw that Tiger was kind of listening and kind of not listening. I didn't know if he'd picked up on what I was saying. But I found out pretty soon.

Tiger was in one of the first foursomes off the tee. When he stepped up, I noticed he was flexing his driver. I thought to myself, "Uh-oh." But then I thought further, "You've got to let these kids learn on their own, and who knows, maybe I'm wrong." Tiger waggled his driver, wound his backswing up, and let fly with a monster of a drive. It was a real boomer down the left center of the fairway, just a little left of the green. It looked like a pretty good shot, but it was farther out there than I would have told him to be ideally. Still, like I was thinking, maybe I was wrong and he was right.

But when Tiger got up to where his ball should've been, there was no ball. Then he saw that there was an asphalt cart path tucked between the fairway and the rough on the left side. The group ahead said Tiger's ball hit the pavement and bounced like flubber up, over the fence, and out of bounds. Tiger just turned around and headed back to the tee.

I stayed where I was so I didn't see what club he took out, but I could tell it was metal, not wood. He hit it out to the right, a little shorter than the first one, with clear access to the green. He played it the way he should have played it the first time.

Later, after the match, I said, "Tiger, you hit a driver on the first hole, didn't you?" He nodded. "Yeah." I said, "Geez, what made you do that? We talked about it in the meeting." He said, "Last time I played here, I hit a driver and it was fine." I said, "When was the last time you played here?" Tiger said, "When I was nine." Neither one of us had to mention that he probably hit the ball a good deal farther at fifteen than at nine.

I'd say he probably learned more from having to walk back to the tee—past the players from the other school, which at the time was the top-ranked team—from not managing the hole the right way, than from any great but lucky shot he might have hit. By the way, on that first hole, Tiger recovered and made a bogey ... which should have been a birdie.

LESSON:
Course Management

A golf course is a piece of geography. It can be surveyed and mapped. Course management is a matter of plotting the most efficient route through the geography. Think of it this way. If you're driving from Boston to San Francisco, you want to take the freeways and interstates, the shortest distance between two points, unless there's construction, in which case you want to find the most efficient way around it. The same applies to a golf hole. In either case, you want the shortest, safest, fastest route. (The trip to San Francisco is just a really, really long par-5.) In either case, make a map before you leave on the trip.

The Trip from Tee to Green

I've broken the process down into five sections, or legs of the trip, from tee to green.

Leg 1—Off the Tee

Bon voyage and godspeed. This is where the journey begins. The better your start, the better your trip. This shot begins the domino effect of golf. Wherever it lands determines your next shot, which determines your next shot, which determines ...

Plan. You're going to hit a tee shot on every hole, every time you play golf. So, you ought to have a plan before you hit it. But the odds are eighteen-to-one you won't. Worse than that, fourteen times you'll automatically reach for your driver and just hit it hard. That's not a plan. That's hoping for the best.

That's what pros *don't* do, just hit without a plan and then hope. Take the 1998 PGA Championship outside of Seattle at

Shahalee Country Club. There were pros who never took their drivers out for the whole week. They looked at each hole differently, not just as a par-4 or -5, but as a separate piece of geography that called for its own different road map from tee to green. True, Shahalee was a tight course with narrow fairways, but, on the other hand, these are the best golfers in the world. If they don't think it's wise to hit a driver off the tee, what makes the rest of us think we should? These pros were hitting three-woods and two-irons, even one-irons (remember, they are pros) so they could get accuracy and control they'd never get with a let-'er-rip driver.

Resist temptation. Admittedly, not reaching for your driver is very hard these days. Especially with all the hype over these supersized, nuclear-powered drivers that we see at pro shops, in magazines, and on infomercials. Once you pay $400 to $500 for a miracle club, you're sure going to want to use it. But those rocket-launchers are supposed to make the ball go 280 yards down the middle, every time. To begin with, few of us hit it right down the middle every time no matter how much we've paid for our driver. Second, many times we don't want the ball to land 280 yards straight in front of where we're standing. How many holes have doglegs at the 175-yard mark? How many have water? What about those big traps or that grove of trees? Do you play short or to the side of that hazard?

What you want is a tee shot that lets you hit your second shot onto or very close to the green. So, you have to look down the fairway and formulate a route before your hand even touches a club in your bag. If it's wide open all the way down, by all means, reach for Big Bertha or Large Larry or Humungus Gus and let it all out.

But your driver isn't the right club if:

1. The hole is a short par-4 and a long drive will put you forty yards off the green when you'd rather be ninety yards off because you hit your long nine-iron better than your short

wedge. Maybe a three-wood or two-iron off the tee would be better.

2. There's a great big lake in the middle of the fairway and you'd rather be in front of it than take a chance on being over it and possibly ending up in it. Maybe a four-wood or three-iron would serve you better than a driver.

3. The fairway makes a sharp left turn but your drives don't hook on demand. Maybe a seven-wood out to the bend and then a long iron to the green is a wiser choice.

Think. The secret weapon is, think before you hit. Lots of us think right after we hit, while the ball is in the air, on its way to the wrong place. That's when the thought flashes across our mind, "Maybe I shouldn't have tried to hit the ball over the top of that small forest of giant redwoods."

Use the whole tee box. It's fifteen to twenty feet wide, but golfer after golfer puts his or her ball down right smack in the middle of the tee box. Golf is a game of angles, like pool only with airborne shots.

Play the angles. If your shots tend to move the ball right to left and there's trouble on the left side of the fairway, tee the ball up in the left third of the box, not in the middle, and for sure, not to the right.

Here's the key. Before you hit the shot, imagine hitting the shot. Knowing how you tend to hit the ball, picture the angle it's likely to travel. How did the picture come out? Did it have a happy ending? If not, adjust your angles. When you're on the tee, it's too late to change the way you hit the ball. But it's not too late to compensate and plan for the way you hit the ball. Use the angles to your advantage. If you hit left to right, compensate. Hit from the right side. Don't hit from the middle and hope that suddenly you won't hit left to right. And don't always hit from the same spot within the tee box. Every hole is different. If there's a hazard, tee up to hit past it. If there are trees, tee up to land in a spot away from them. Same goes for water and sand. They're not moving, so you better.

USE THE WHOLE TEE BOX
FOR BEST ANGLE

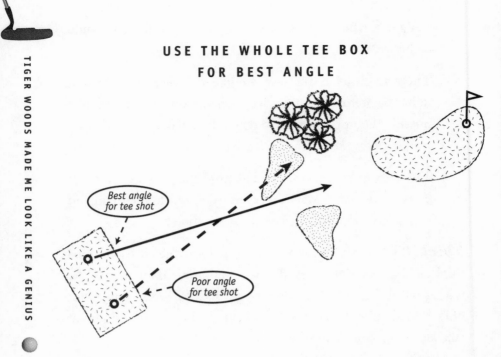

Best angle for tee shot

Poor angle for tee shot

About doglegs. If you come to a hole that goes straight out for 200 yards and then takes a left turn, you need a plan. Many golfers can hit a drive over 200 yards. Let's say you hit it 225 on that dogleg left. You're already in trouble, i.e. trees, water, out-of-bounds. If the hole turns to the right, move to the left so you're hitting to the widest part of the turn. When you see out-of-bounds down the left side of the fairway, tee up from the left side of the tee box and give yourself the best chance to hit the ball in bounds.

So, do you hit the ball to the left or right? That depends on two things: How big the trouble is and how you happen to hit the ball. Let's say the dogleg is a gentle left turn, around a small clump of bushes, with lots of fairway to the right, and you happen to hit with a draw from right to left. Then you can aim right, hit a full driver, and let the ball make the turn. On the other hand, if the hole doglegs to the right, your 225-yard right-to-left draw is going to take you away from where the fairway is headed and into trouble, more than likely a trap, rough, or the dreaded out-of-bounds.

Alternatives. Here's where you think through other ways to get where you're going. Maybe a three-wood or five-wood, which will travel a little less distance, so even with your draw, it will leave you in the wide part of the fairway as the hole makes its turn. Or, if you're like most golfers, your irons draw less and travel straighter. You could hit a nice straight two- or three-iron, tight to the corner, still leaving you with an open shot to the green, still putting you in par position. Think about the way you hit the ball nine out of ten times and determine how to best use that shot on the geography in front of you. Make the mathematically wise choice.

Don't roll the dice. One thing you should not do is assume that despite the fact that you draw the ball right to left nine out of ten times, this one time in ten you'll make a slight adjustment and not draw it right to left. That's an adjustment that Tiger might make, though not often. But the rest of us don't have such accurate dials on our swings, stances, and grips. It's ten-to-one against us.

Don't automatically reach for your driver just because you're on the tee. In fact, automatically stop yourself before you reach for your driver. Only use it when it makes sense.

Plan to make a plan. I know I said make a plan already. But I can't stress this enough. Don't leave for a trip without a map. Don't buy your map along the road to get you out of trouble you're already in. Learn about the course before you play it. Ask other players. Look at the scorecard. It's an encyclopedia of information if you read it thoroughly. Check the course distance and par, the hole distances, hole-by-hole handicap ratings, the number of par 5s and par 3s.

Don't Give Your Opponent the Advantage of Knowing More Than You Do

In Tiger's senior year, he was playing in the California Interscholastic Federation finals at La Cumbre Country Club. The rules were, you couldn't play the course, or even walk the course, for a week or two in advance of the tournament.

But that didn't stop us from pursuing course management. We were at the course on the Sunday before the play started on Monday. Through a friend of mine, I had found a book that told about some of the holes, what to watch for and where the trouble would be waiting. I showed the book to Tiger, and we took it with us while we drove around the outside of the course. It's kind of an odd course that winds around and doesn't have many bushes or any fences, so you can actually see a lot of the layout of several holes. We compared what we saw on the course to what we'd seen and read in the book.

We were starting to get a feel for the golf course when I noticed, in my rearview mirror, a van following us. I didn't think anything of it at first. We weren't breaking any rules, and I couldn't imagine someone mistaking me for a spy.

Pretty soon, we had covered all the holes we could and I drove back to the clubhouse. I turned down what I thought was a little road from the parking lot toward the driving range. It was actually just a wide cart path. I think Tiger knew it, but he didn't say anything. The next thing I knew, I had driven down this path, right up to the range, which was only about ten practice tees wide. I realized I'd better get out of there. When I looked in the mirror to back up, there was the van, right behind us. I was in my wife's little Integra, so I maneuvered pretty well. But the van, which was about twice the size of my car, was having a tough time trying to turn around. When we drove by them, I could look right into their window.

It was Terry Noe, who was going to be the next Junior Amateur Champion after Tiger, and his dad. They'd been following us around, making sure that everything we knew about the course, they'd know. We couldn't blame them. But we did laugh at them trying to do a U-turn in the cart path.

Assess each hole from the tee. Look down the fairway and estimate the yardage to the first sign of trouble, a bunker or a dogleg. Check left and right for fairway width to see how much forgiveness the hole offers. Look at that cute carved diagram of the hole that's usually on a rustic piece of wood next to the ball-washer. It's not just there for charm, it's a map. It shows the danger spots—the bends, the traps, the streams, the rough, the boundaries—and the safest route to where you're headed.

USE THE "MAP" AT EACH TEE

After you've absorbed all the information available and matched it with the way you hit the ball and your options, make a plan for the hole and play it. Don't worry, you won't slow the game down. You can do it while washing your ball, writing down the score, or listening to another player mutter about his "shouldas" and "couldas" from the last hole.

Aim. Pick out where you want the ball to land—a target, not just a general area called "out there." Think. Then use the part of the tee box that gives you the best chance of landing your target. You have five hundred to seven hundred square feet in the tee box, the equivalent of a medium-size family room. Use all of it.

Learn. If you plan your shot and it doesn't go where you planned, chances are it will be close. It might be in the right direction but a little short. Or long. Maybe right or left. But at least you had a plan. You learned something about the hole and the course that you can use next time. If you didn't plan the shot, the only way it can go where you want is by accident. Chances are it will go somewhere you don't want it to go. And you'll have learned nothing you can use next time you play.

Leg 2—Your Second Shot on Par Fives

With an average of two par 5s per nine, you're probably going to hit this shot about four times. Assuming you're not going to hit the green in two on a par 5, where do you want to be when you hit your third shot? The second shot is critically important in setting up where and how you play that third shot. That's your short game, the strokes that will take your ball all the way into the cup. If the second shot puts you in a good position, you can get down in three more for a par. If not, you're taking unnecessary strokes.

By the way, the second shot on a par 5 is virtually the same as your first shot on a short par 4. It sets up your approach to the green shot. The same lessons apply.

Your favorite club. In both instances, par 5 or short par 4, you have the opportunity to put yourself in position to hit your favorite club in the bag. If yours is a pitching wedge from eighty yards, aim to land eighty yards out from the green. If your favorite is a full nine-iron from one hundred yards, plan your shots accordingly. This is one of your rare chances to play the hole to your best advantage, not the hole's. After all, you've been at the range practicing. You know what you're good at. Use it.

Sometimes Everything Works

The first hole at Dad Miller, our home course during Tiger's first year at Western, was a 307-yard par-4. It was a classic example of your first shot on a short par 4 being like your second shot on a par 5. It's the place to apply the lesson: Use your favorite club off the tee; don't just reach for your driver.

Even in his freshman year, we already had crowds gathering to watch Tiger to see if he was as good as the rumors reported. When he stepped up to the first hole in a match against Edison, the crowd got what it came for. Tiger didn't reach for his driver. He chose one of his favorite clubs, his three-wood. His plan was to hit the ball to a spot that would give him the best access to the green. His driver might give him distance but not necessarily the control he needed.

Well, he got just what he needed and more. There was a reason his three-wood was such a favorite. He hit it nearly as far as his driver but with more accuracy, in this case, right in front of the green . . . and, with a little bonus roll, onto the green about six feet from the hole. Then he sunk his putt for an eagle two!

Okay, now will you believe me when I tell you not to automatically reach for your driver just because you're on the tee?

Calculate. Use simple math to pick your clubs. Let's say the hole is a 300-yard par-4, like the one Tiger played. To get back to reality, in your case, say you want to be 90 yards off the green so you can hit a three-quarter wedge for your second shot. If your driver usually goes 225 to 235 yards, add that to 90, and you're over the hole by 15 to 25 yards. Don't hit the driver. Try the three-wood.

If the hole is a 525-yard par-5 and you want to be 100 yards out to hit your favorite nine-iron, you've got two shots to cover 425 yards. You can hit your driver for 225 and a strong three-iron or an easy four-wood for the rest. Or you can tee off with the three-wood and hit another three-wood from the fairway. Just do the calculation and pick the clubs you hit best in order to make the distance.

Don't go for broke. They call it "broke" for a reason. Don't hit the ball as far as you possibly can. Too many times, we step up to a long par 5 and talk ourselves into thinking this is the one time we're going to make the green in two. Same goes for the short par 4 we convince ourselves we're going to hit from the tee. Frequently there's a small family of traps surrounding the green or a placid little pond filled with fish and Titleists. If you don't make the green, and even if you don't land in the hazards, you're still going to have a thirty- to forty-yard chip shot from the front, side, or back of the green, one of the most difficult distances in the game. You're always better off 75 to 110 yards out or right on the fringe, not in between.

Play smart. Just because it is theoretically possible—on the perfect day, with the perfect shots, the wind at your back, the earth's gravitational pull at its geophysical low point, the ghost of Ben Hogan watching over you, and a good fortune cookie the night before—to hit the par 5 in two or the par 4 with your drive, doesn't mean it's smart golf.

> **Smart golf isn't hitting the ball far,
> it's hitting the ball less often.**

Shot management adds up to course management. Why hit a long drive and an all-you've-got three-wood on a par 5 and hope the ball gets to the green or stays out of trouble? Manage your shots in advance. After your drive, make your second shot a five-wood or three-iron so you leave the ball 90 yards off the green. On a par 4, why even use the driver when you can manage your shots with a five-wood and a wedge? Put yourself in position to hit the shot you like to hit, not one you have to hit. If you manage every shot, pretty soon you've managed the hole, and eventually the course.

Leg 3—Your Second Shot on Par 4s or Your First Shot on Par 3s

Add these up and they amount to a shot you'll hit on all but six or seven holes, or up to twelve times in a round of golf. Since this shot can put you on or at least very close to the green, it can be a real stroke-saver. Once your ball is on the green, you should be left with no more than two strokes for a par. Even if your ball is only near the green, you have good a chance to chip close and one- or two-putt for a par and no worse than a bogey. However, if you don't plan it carefully, the same shot could leave you right, left, or over and looking at extra strokes.

INSIGHT:
Take a Tip from the Pros

Here's a place to learn from the best in the game, particularly when they're playing in the major tournaments—the U.S. Open, the British Open, the Masters, the PGA. The courses have purposely been made as hard as possible to give the pros the ultimate challenge and provide the public with the most entertainment. They have to play smart to beat those courses.

In contrast, look at how they can play in the secondary tournaments or the charity events. Those golf courses haven't been set up to torture them, so the really good players can just let out the shaft on their drives, hit wedges to the greens, and putt for birdies all day. The winners and low finishers of those tournaments can end up twenty under par.

Back to the majors. These courses are turned from tough to downright mean, with traps dug deep, the rough like a jungle, fairways narrowed to one-lane roads, and pins hidden behind bunkers on the downhill slopes of close-cut greens. Instead of finishing way under par, a good score is even par or one over. A great score is a couple under. The promoters want the pros to struggle. It makes for better endings and better television.

Aim for that big green oval. That tournament course still has say, ten par 4s and three par 3s, but now the par 3s are almost like par 4s and the 4s are like par 4-and-a-halfs. So what do the pros do? They shoot for the green more than for the pin. If a pro can hit a second shot on a difficult par 4 onto the green, then he can knock a putt in for a birdie or sink it in two for a par. But, if he'd have gone for the pin that was teetering over the trap and missed, he'd be hitting his third shot out of sand.

Ignore the pin. The amateur, me and you, should be thinking the same way on the course every day. Those courses are tough enough for us before some promoter starts hiding flags and making the fairways skinnier. Often the pin is in a place where you're better off not even looking. If it's next to a trap, take the trap out of play. If it's near water, mentally move to dry land. Create your own pin in the center of the green. Aim there, hit there, and putt from there.

Think about it as a geometry problem. How far can the pin be from the center? At most, only as far as the radius of the green, and most likely less. You've been practicing your putting. You can get down in two from there, maybe even one.

Listen to the pros talking to the sportscasters and interviewers at the end of a challenging tournament. Over and over, you hear that line, "I just kept hitting to the middle of the greens." Usually, it's the one in the winner's blazer who's saying the line.

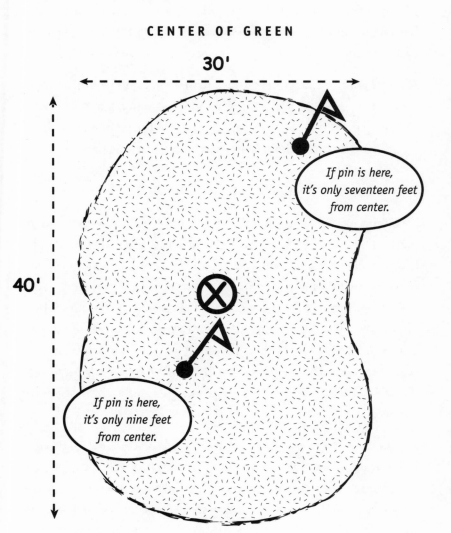

CENTER OF GREEN

30'

40'

If pin is here, it's only seventeen feet from center.

If pin is here, it's only nine feet from center.

The club that gets you to the green. Before you pick your club for that second shot on a par 4 or first shot on a par 3, think about the distance you're hitting. If you're at the 150-yard marker, remember, the distance isn't to the pin, it's to the center of the green. That's all the more reason to aim for the center and select the best club to get you to the center. The pros get a pin sheet, a guide that tells them how long each hole is, factoring in where the pin has been placed on each green. Even with that information, they often hit for the middle of the green. So, select the club that will take the ball 150 yards, to the middle of the green.

Exceptions. Some golfers, those with a ten handicap or less, can look at the green like a pie, cut into four pieces, and aim for the slice closest to the pin. But even then, think about the pros in the majors. Do it if you feel confident. Otherwise, use the whole pie.

Leg 4—Long Par 3s

The long par 3 is entirely different than a short or average-length par 3. These are two hundred yards or more, often surrounded by traps, water, bunkers, and, on a bad day, Ninja warriors. These holes are just daring you to try to hit your tee shot perfectly—over, under, and through the maze of evils that lay in wait—and somehow land your ball on the green and roll up within a few feet of the pin. These are machismo-testers. To men, I say, get in touch with your feminine side. To women, I usually don't have to say anything. They're not trying to prove anything, just get a good score on the hole.

Be like an astronaut. Find a safe place to land. Hit your tee shot to a good, approachable position, chip well, and get your par through cunning and skill, not testosterone. Even if you settle for a bogey, somebody in your foursome (inevitably a male—God, we're stubborn) will have tried to bring the hole to its knees and find himself at the near side of the pond, bidding good-bye to his ball and dropping a brand new one, whimpering, "In in one, out in two, shooting three."

Think of it as an easy par 4. Just give yourself a little attitude adjustment and you'll play these holes much smarter and much better. If the scorecard called the hole a par 4 but said it was only

230 yards long, you'd feel very confident about your chances of making that four for par. Hit a long ball that puts you close to the green, chip on, two-putt, and you've made par. But when it's called a par 3, suddenly you feel the pressure to go for the green on your tee shot. The green is surrounded by trouble, which you now find yourself in, rather than in front of or next to, and you're looking at a double or triple bogie or worse.

Accuracy, not distance. Pick your club based on the imaginary, easy par 4. Don't use your driver or even your three-wood. Think about a five-wood or three-iron. Go for accuracy over distance. Put the ball in the open area between those two traps that guard the green, or just in front of the water, say twenty-five to thirty yards short of the green, in good position to chip close to the hole.

This is why you practice chipping and putting. Once you get that close, you may just birdie that easy par 4—that is, make par on the par 3. Pitch aggressively, get near the pin, putt for the back of the cup, and you've got a realistic chance to score well. If you don't, you've made a respectable bogey four. And you have no chance of being in real trouble and ruining a perfectly good round just because you tried to flex your muscles instead of your brain.

Leg 5—Around the Green

Most golfers, when they're finally close enough to get a good look at the pin, stop seeing. They don't note the undulations or slopes on the green; they don't check for short grass, long grass, bald spots, or moisture. They don't see what's right in front of them. My advice? Open your eyes. View the rest of the hole as a par 2. Where are the hazards? What do you do to get around them? How do you get down in par from wherever the ball sits?

Did I mention, have a plan? Don't just chip and hope. Observe, think, plan. Where do you want the ball to be? How do you get it there? That depends on the situation:

- **If the green is relatively flat** . . . do what you've been doing at the practice range. Loft the ball toward the hole with a pitching wedge, going for the imaginary three-foot half circle around the back of the hole. Yes, you're trying to put the chip shot in the cup. That's not unrealistic. It's very possible, and trying to do it is the best way to put the ball in one-putt range.

- **If the green is sloped and you're chipping up from below the hole** . . . you don't want to chip past the hole. That can leave you putting on the Olympic downhill slalom course. You have to plan the distance of your chip so that it stops on the front side of the cup, still leaving you with an uphill putt. That means you don't need backspin on the ball. You want the ball to land in front of the pin with topspin to keep it rolling closer to the hole.

- **If the green is sloped and you're chipping down from above the hole** . . . you can be (carefully) aggressive. What that means is, it's okay if your ball ends up past the hole leaving you with an uphill putt, as long as it's not too far past the hole. When you're chipping downhill, the green is going to give you all the roll you need. If you run a six- or eight-iron, you won't have to hit it much, the green will do most of the work. If you loft it with a wedge, the club's backspin will be somewhat offset by the green's slope, so again, you don't have to give it much.

- **If the green rolls (and most of them do)** . . . study it before you chip. Take an extra second and step onto the green. See where the undulations are and where the plateaus occur. See where the sharp drops level off. Then find a specific spot where you want your ball to land. Don't just hit. Aim and then hit. Even if you miss your spot, you miss by a limited amount and you're in the same area. If you don't aim, you end up who-knows-where.

TIGER, AFTER COURSE MANAGEMENT

This story took place a good deal later in the year than the Recreation Park lesson. This one took place on what was then our home course, Dad Miller, in Anaheim. The 8th hole there is a short par-5 that narrows down pretty tight in a couple of places. There's an out-of-bounds on the left and big, mean trees all along on the right. When you get to around the 250-yard mark, there's a nice big opening, but just past there, at about 270, the fairway narrows again, between the out-of-bounds and the trees, down to maybe 25 to 30 yards in width. It's like a little skinny neck on a guy with steroid shoulders.

This hole was a course management lesson every time you played it. Plenty of kids, seeing that wide opening 250 yards out there, would pull out their drivers. It wasn't so bad if they hit it poorly. The hole forgives you most of the way down. The bad news would come if they hit it good. They'd get a little roll and then they'd be in deep trouble in the trees or, worse, out of bounds.

Tiger didn't use his driver on number eight. Never, as I recall. He used a one- or two-iron. Inevitably, he'd land in that wide-open expanse midway down the fairway, with a 190- to 200-yard, clear, clean shot to the green. For him, that meant a five- or six-iron, clubs that he hit long and straight all day, every day. He loved those middle irons, and he seemed to be able to put them right where he wanted them. (Remember what I said about putting yourself in position to hit your favorite club, not the club the hole makes you hit?) Meanwhile, his teammates and opponents were trying to crush drives off the tee and then trying to dig themselves out of trouble on their second shots.

Tiger probably birdied that hole more times than he parred it. That's course management. Shot by shot, hole by hole.

Crosby's Quick Refresher
CROSBY FOUR–COURSE MANAGEMENT

INSIGHT: *The only constant on the golf course is the golf course.*

> **Smart golf isn't hitting the ball far,**
> **it's hitting the ball less often.**

LESSON: *Course Management—the Trip from Tee to Green*

- **Leg 1—Off the Tee**
  - Plan.
  - Resist "driver temptation."
  - Use whole tee box and play the angles.
  - Doglegs:
    - Look for alternatives, hit short, hit to open area.
    - Don't gamble, play your best game, aim, learn from experience.

- **Leg 2—Second Shot, par 5s**
  - Calculate yardage, assess best club.
  - A chance to use your favorite club, club you hit best.
  - Don't go for broke, play smart, manage each shot.

- **Leg 3—Second Shot, par 4s, and first shot, par 3s**
  - Aim for the green, ignore the pin.
  - Use the club that gets you to the green.

- **Leg 4—Long Par 3s**
  - Think "easy par 4"—accuracy, not distance.
  - Find a safe place to land.
  - Practice chipping and putting to make par, not long tee shot.

- **Leg 5—Around Green**
  - If flat, go for hole.
  - If sloped up with ball below, chip below to putt aggressively.
  - If sloped down with ball above, chip aggressively (doesn't take much).
  - Read the roll like putting.

Stats.
Find out what needs work.
Work on it.

INSIGHT:
Not Knowing Your Stats Is a Handicap

Most golfers know their handicaps. Unfortunately, that's usually the only statistic they know about their game. Ask them how many three-putt greens they average or if they generally get more bogeys than double-bogeys and they scrunch up their foreheads trying to remember the last round they played.

On the other hand, ask any NCAA coach how his football team is doing and he'll answer you in numbers: completions, ground gains, third-down conversions, kick returns, interceptions, sacks, possession time. Baseball fans can recite the batting averages, RBIs, ERAs, bunts, walks, and steals of twenty or thirty players. They know when a slugger is in a slump and how many percentage points it has hurt his average. A WNBA player will analyze her game by category. She'll tell you, "I'm 65 percent from the line," and while she's saying that, she's probably bouncing a ball, lining up free throws in practice. Even high school ballplayers and Little Leaguers know their numbers.

Why? Because stats matter. They identify what needs attention in your game. It's not enough to say you're off your game or your score isn't good. You have to know why. It's unlikely that everything is going wrong. You may be hitting well off the tee but not chipping with accuracy. You could be having trouble with your long irons but coming out of the sand pretty well. Maybe your long putts are on the money but you're having difficulty inside three feet. You have to find out what's wrong before you can fix it. Stats are the diagnosis that tells you what to treat.

LESSON:
How to Keep Your Stats

1. Use your scorecard for more than your score. It's a snapshot of every aspect of your last round, from tee to green, not just the number of strokes you took.

2. Keep a scorecard of your scorecards. From round to round, patterns will emerge. You'll find out what you're good at, what needs work, and what will result in the greatest improvement to your game.

The Crosby Card: Not Just a Score, But a Reference Book on Each Round

Next time you play, don't keep a scorecard the way you always have. Don't just finish the hole and jot down your score, then move on to the next hole, and every nine add them up. At best, all that tells you is your birdies, pars, bogeys, and double-bogeys, and how you did versus the course's par. For most golfers, it tells them even less, just a number: 45 or 52 or 41. *Better than last time. Worse than last time. Good enough to beat the other person.* That's not enough.

I tell my players to make the scorecard an encyclopedia of information, which I humbly call the Crosby Card. Collect all your data from the hole, enter it, and review it. Look at the box the scorecard provides for each hole. It's a simple square, but there's room for a lot more than just a number.

- CENTER—number of strokes per hole. When you finish the hole, put your score—say, a "5"—in the middle of the box as you always do, but from now on, make it a little smaller. Then use the four corners of the box for more information.

- UPPER LEFT CORNER—fairway (or not). In the upper left corner, put an "f" if your tee shot landed in the fairway. This usually applies to fourteen of eighteen holes, since the average course has four par 3s. (You don't really consider par 3s to have fairways since you're supposed to hit the green with your tee shot.)

  Details. If you want, you can add nuances to your notation. For example, if you put the ball in the fairway and in the position you wanted, you can use a capital "F" rather than of a lowercase "f." On the other hand, you can put an "r" if your shot went into the rough or an "o" if it went out of bounds. This can prove to be valuable later on.

- **UPPER RIGHT CORNER**—green. If you hit the green on a par 4 in two, you're on in "regulation." Put a dot —•—in the upper right-hand corner of the score box. If you're on the green in three on a par 5, give yourself a dot. And if your tee shot is on the green of a par three, put in a dot. If you get on in less than regulation—say in two on a par 5—put an extra little circle around the dot.

- **LOWER LEFT CORNER**—traps. If you're in a trap rather than on the green, use the lower left-hand corner to indicate how you did. Put a little circle—○—in the corner. If you get out and on the green in one shot from the trap, put a "1"

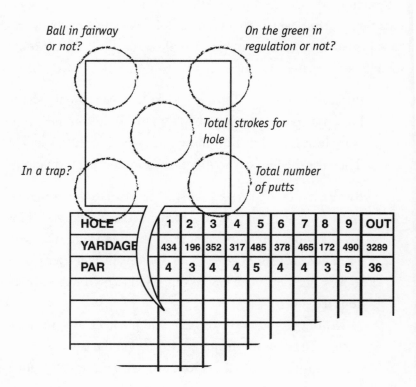

Ball in fairway or not?

On the green in regulation or not?

Total strokes for hole

In a trap?

Total number of putts

HOLE	1	2	3	4	5	6	7	8	9	OUT
YARDAGE	434	196	352	317	485	378	465	172	490	3289
PAR	4	3	4	4	5	4	4	3	5	36

inside the little circle. If it took you two or three shots to get out, put that number inside the circle.

- **LOWER RIGHT CORNER**—putts. In the lower right hand corner, write down how many putts you took once your ball was on the green. If you two-putted, put a "2" in the lower right corner. (Don't count it if you use your putter from the fringe for an approach shot. Only record the actual strokes on the putting surface.) This will not only keep track of the absolute number of putts per hole and per round, but will also give you the all-important number of three-putt greens. Working on getting rid of those is one of the quickest ways to reduce your score.

When you're all done, your scorecard box should look something like this:

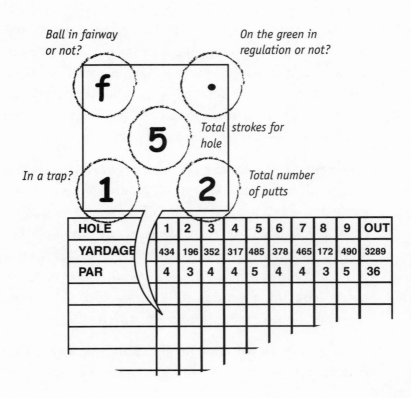

Ball in fairway or not?

On the green in regulation or not?

Total strokes for hole

In a trap?

Total number of putts

HOLE	1	2	3	4	5	6	7	8	9	OUT
YARDAGE	434	196	352	317	485	378	465	172	490	3289
PAR	4	3	4	4	5	4	4	3	5	36

What Can You Learn from Scoring a Round This Way?

1. *You know your score.* But your score by itself only tells you, in total, how well you played that day. You shot 44 and 46 for a 90. That's eighteen shots over par and, let's say, a couple of shots better than your average game. A score of eighteen over is bogey golf, which could mean good, consistent play or could mean a day of extremes—double-bogeys offset by birdies. There's a big difference. One way indicates you've gotten your game together and the other suggests the opposite. That's where the Crosby Card helps. It points to where you did well and where you wasted shots.

2. *You know how many fairways you hit.* That tells you if you put your ball in good enough position in the fairways to make pars, or if you were in the rough (or worse) and faced with bogeys or double-bogeys. It also indicates whether you were able to take advantage of good fairway position by getting on the green in regulation (the next piece of information). Add up the number of dots and compare it with the number of pars. Don't be surprised to see a correlation. (And if you don't see one, look at your number of putts.)

3. *You know if you hit the green in regulation.* That's a sure predictor of par. Count the number of greens you reached in regulation and see how many you parred. Most, right? If you didn't, you're narrowing your focus of practice down to the putting green. Count the number of greens that you didn't hit in regulation. Look at your scores on those holes. Now think back to the clubs you used on your approach shots. Those are the ones that need attention.

4. *In case you could ever forget, now you know how many traps you were in.* More important, you know how

many strokes it took to get out. If you're spending more than one shot to get out and on the green, it's time find a practice sand trap again, get that two-by-four, and go back to work.

5. *You know exactly how many putts you took.* You know how many two-putt greens you had. Ideally, the answer should be eighteen, unless you one-putted. You know how many three-putt greens you had. And, if you had any, how many four-putt greens. That tells you two things. First, how close were your chip shots? If you're consistently left with twenty-five- to-thirty-five-foot putts, go back and "chip away at your score." Second, how well are you doing with your short putts—the two-to-three-footers? You should be able to count on making those. The putt corner of the scorecard tells the last, and pivotal, chapter in the story of each hole.

The Master Card: Your
Scorecard of Scorecards

Okay, that's one round. You may play altogether differently tomorrow. That's why you need to keep a scorecard of scorecards. I call it Crosby's Master Card—you get "credit" for what you did right and you "pay" for what you did wrong. Here's how it works:

Every time you play, you keep your scorecard, as I explained. Then you take the information from each scorecard and enter it onto an overall scorecard that you keep over several months. You can set it up like a spreadsheet on your computer, or you can keep it by hand. Lay it out like this (see following page):

DATE	GOLF COURSE	PAR	SCORE	OVER/ UNDER PAR	
NAME					
TOTAL					
AVERAGE					

As you can see, I break all my stats into nine-hole rounds, not eighteen. It's a little easier to get a snapshot of your game in nine-hole segments. So, once you finish playing, you go home, take out your Crosby Card with all the relevant data, and enter that data onto your Master Card. Just move across the sheet, from left to right, filling in each column.

		3					
	PUTTS	PUTTS	BIRDIES	PARS	BOGIES	DB+	GREENS

- **DATE**—Fill in the date so you can track your progress over time.

- **COURSE**—This is important because there's more to course differences than just what par happens to be. Some courses will fit your style, others won't. You'll learn if you play better on long or short courses, hilly, flat, hazardous, or whatever.

- **PAR**—This is your benchmark. Enter it nine holes at a time—say 36. If you played eighteen holes, just repeat the course name and add an "F" or a "B" to indicate front nine or back nine.

- **SCORE**—This one is obvious. How did you score, round by round? Enter your nine-hole score—for instance, 44.

- **OVER/UNDER PAR**—This is your first piece of important information. If par is 36 and you shot 44, you were eight over. As you add rounds, throughout the season, you'll be able to track your improvement.

- **PUTTS**—Add up the total putts per nine holes from the lower right corner of the boxes on your scorecards. Maybe you had nineteen. Right away, you know you're aiming for no more than eighteen, so you've got one too many.

- **THREE PUTTS +**—This is a very important statistic. How many three-putt (or more) greens did you have last round? Let's say two. That means to have made only nineteen putts, you had to one-putt one green. One-putts are nice, but they're not something you can count on, so you still want to work on those three-putt greens. As you play more rounds, check your three-putt progress. Are you having fewer of them as the season goes on?

- **BIRDIES**—How many birdies did you get in nine holes? Let's say one. Good. But did you get the full benefit of the birdie by lowering your total score, or did it have to make up for a hole where you expended extra shots? A couple of columns to the right will tell you that story.

- **PARS**—These are your goal. How many did you achieve out of your last nine? If you were eight over par, chances are, one or two. Enter your pars and watch them round by round.

- **BOGEYS**—Okay, a good steady bogey golfer who scores eight over for nine holes should have mostly bogeys. Did you? Or did you get to your score by occasional brilliance (birdies and pars) offsetting intermittent disasters (double-bogeys or worse)? The answers are all there on the Master Card.

- **DOUBLE-BOGEYS +**—These are your nemesis. Every time you get a double-bogey or more, you have to work extra hard, or get extra lucky, to make up for it. Most of us just can't afford to have to recover from too many double- or triple-bogeys in a round. If all you did is get rid of half of your double-bogeys in a season, think how much you could improve your score.

- **GREENS**—How many did you hit in regulation? Technically, one would be okay for a bogey golfer (if every other shot was played without a problem). Hitting none of your greens in regulation means trouble. Three or four means you're getting to where you need to be—the green—just fine, but once you're there, your putting may not be delivering for you. Look back at your "Putts" column to see where the answer lies.

Totals and Averages

Now you've filled in your first nine-hole round on your Master Card. Fill in the next and the next, each time you play. Then, at the bottom, keep running totals. These totals tell the truth about your game. They balance out the fluke rounds where you played better or worse than usual; the day you could do nothing but three-putt but made up for it by holing out a chip shot and hitting a green in less than regulation; the one, glorious day when you hit every fairway and thought you'd never have to work on tee shots again. The numbers tell you, on average, how you play, and what needs attention. You might have shot 40 last time out, which is only four over par, but you're averaging 44, which is eight over. On the other hand, you may have taken 22 putts in a recent round but, in general, you're taking 17.5. Your putting is really strong despite one off day.

Improvement

Study the totals and averages. They are a diagnosis, telling you what part of your game needs treatment. As the year or season goes on, they indicate whether you're making progress. And they tell you what to work on next. Don't look at your raw score alone. Look at each component that went into your score. Your game improves piece by piece, shot by shot. Finally, after a couple of months of treating the areas in need, look at your average score. When you improve the parts, the whole will follow.

THE BRYON BELL STORY—FROM A 20+ HANDICAP TO A 14 (NOT EVERYONE IS TIGER)

When I say stats can tell the story of your golf game, I mean that literally. Take a look at some of the Master Cards of my players. The closer you look, the more you'll see patterns emerge that reveal the type of player, as well as the player's areas of vulnerability and improvement. By studying another player's stats, you may see parallels with areas of your own game that need attention.

Look at the story the stats tell of Bryon Bell as a freshman at Western in 1991, the same year Tiger was a freshman. (The big difference—Bryon was a 20+ handicapper.)

Bryon had a good basic swing, and he was a very intelligent kid. Every couple of weeks we reviewed his stats, and he could see what needed his attention. If you compare his freshman stats with his sophomore stats, you'll see very dramatic improvement in key elements of his game.

Bryon averaged 19.1 putts per nine holes in 1991. By the end of 1992, he had brought that down to 15.8, a difference of 3.3 strokes per nine holes. That's big! How did it happen? The old-fashioned way. Bryon putted and putted and putted. He did the drills from inside two feet. He putted for the back of the hole. He played the Pullback Game and the Too Bad Game until he wasn't the one pulling back or hearing "too bad."

Look at the effect all the putting practice had on his three-putt greens. In 1991, he averaged 2.4 three putts per nine holes, but by the end of '92 he was down to just 1.0 per nine.

Some areas that didn't need as much focus were left alone to allow time for those that needed extra diligence. For example, he had 0.1 birdies in '91 and 0.3 in '92. Bryon, at this stage of his game, was not a birdie player. He shouldn't have been looking to pick up a whole lot more birdies; it would have been wishful thinking, and it probably would have caused him to take unnecessary risks, ultimately costing him strokes. Instead, he concentrated on the potential weaknesses, double- and triple-bogeys.

Initially, Bryon was making more double-bogeys than bogeys. He simply couldn't afford to keep doing that. In his freshman year, he averaged 3.6 double- or triple-bogeys per nine. That's three to six essentially wasted strokes. By the close of his sophomore season, he had the number down to an average of 2.4 per nine.

What happened was, Bryon and I analyzed his game and determined *why* he was making double-bogeys. We counted how many fairways he hit, worked on selecting the right club from the tee, and then he hit those clubs over and over on the practice range. He worked on the clubs and shots that cut down the strokes before he got to the green—the middle and short irons. In the one area of double-bogeys, Bryon saved himself between one and three shots per nine. He got to the point where he made more bogeys than double-bogeys, reversing a situation that was the core of his problem.

Even his pars improved along the way. He only averaged 1.8 per nine in '91, but was up to 2.9 in '92, better than a full-stroke

| BRYON BELL–1991 | | | | OVER | |
DATE	GOLF COURSE/OPPONENT	PAR	SCORE	PAR	
2/19/91	DAD MILLER	34	46	12	
2/20/91	DM	34	49	15	
2/21/91	DM	34	46	12	
2/25/91	DM	34	42	8	
2/26/91	RECREATION PARK	36	48	12	
3/4/91	DM	34	49	15	
3/6/91	RECREATION PARK	36	52	15	
3/11/91	DM	34	43	9	
3/14/91	DM	34	46	12	
3/18/91	DM	34	42	8	
3/19/91	SEACLIFF	36	55	14	
4/1/91	DM	34	50	16	
4/2/91	DM	34	45	11	
4/4/91	DM	34	45	11	
4/8/91	MEADOWLARK/MARINA	35	43	8	
4/9/91	IMPERIAL/BREA	37	57	20	
4/10/91	DM/MAGNOLIA	34	41	7	
4/15/91	DM/LA QUINTA	34	47	13	
4/17/91	FULLERTON/SERVITE	33	49	16	
4/18/91	ALTA VISTA/VALENCIA	37	56	19	
4/22/91	MILESQUARE/LA QUINTA	36	49	13	
4/23/91	DM/SAVANNA	34	44	10	
4/24/91	DM/MAGNOLIA	34	41	7	
4/25/91	DM/BREA	34	42	8	
4/26/91	CATALINA/SERVITE	32	41	9	
TOTAL		862	1168	300	
AVERAGE		34.5	46.7	12.0	

improvement. Bottom line, look at his average score. In 1991, Bryon Bell generally shot 46.7 for nine holes. In 1992, his typical score dropped to 43.4 for nine. He improved the parts and his score followed.

PUTTS	3 PUTTS	BIRDIES	PARS	BOGIES	DB+	GREENS
18	1	0	1	5	3	1
19	3	0	0	4	5	1
21	2	0	2	3	4	2
19	1	1	3	2	3	2
22	4	0	0	4	5	0
22	4	0	2	2	5	1
22	4	0	2	2	5	1
16	0	0	3	5	1	1
18	2	0	1	5	3	2
18	2	0	4	2	3	0
18	2	0	0	5	4	0
22	5	0	0	4	5	2
17	1	1	1	3	4	2
20	3	0	1	5	3	2
17	2	0	3	5	1	3
20	2	0	1	2	6	1
18	3	0	5	1	3	2
23	5	0	1	4	4	3
19	1	0	1	3	5	1
20	3	0	0	1	8	0
14	1	0	1	5	3	0
17	2	0	1	6	2	2
20	3	0	3	5	1	4
16	1	0	4	2	3	2
21	3	0	4	3	2	5
477	60	2	44	88	91	40
19.1	2.4	0.1	1.8	3.5	3.6	1.6

| BRYON BELL–1992 | | | | OVER | |
DATE	GOLF COURSE/OPPONENT	PAR	SCORE	PAR	
3/4/92	LA MIRADA/GAHR	35	43	8	
3/9/92	RECREATION PARK/POLY	36	43	7	
3/10/92	MESA VERDE/ESTANCIA	36	56	20	
3/11/92	LOS COYOTES/POLY	36	47	11	
3/12/92	SEACLIFF/EDISON	36	51	15	
3/16/92	DM/EDISON	35	40	5	
3/17/92	YORBA LINDA/ESPERANZA	35	44	9	
3/18/92	LOS COYOTES/ESPERANZA	36	48	12	
3/19/92	LOS COYOTES/LA QUINTA	36	45	9	
3/23/92	MILESQUARE/LA QUINTA	36	45	9	
3/24/92	LOS COYOTES/LB WILSON	36	43	7	
3/26/92	ALTA VISTA/VALENCIA	37	49	12	
3/30/92	RECREATION PARK/WILSON	36	42	6	
3/31/92	DM/SAVANNA	35	40	5	
4/2/92	LOS COYOTES/BREA	36	43	7	
4/6/92	MEADOWLARK/MARINA	35	47	12	
4/7/92	LOS COYOTES/MAGNOLIA	36	42	6	
4/8/92	LOS COYOTES/ESTANCIA-GAHR	36	43	7	
4/10/92	SKYLINKS/AVALON	36	47	11	
4/13/92	WSI/RANCHO CANADA-E	35	42	7	
		36	46	10	
4/14/92	WSI/RANCHO CANADA-W	36	43	7	
		35	44	9	
4/20/92	DM/MARINA	35	38	3	
4/21/92	ALTA VISTA/CORONA	37	37	0	
4/22/92	LOS COYOTES/VALENCIA	36	48	12	
4/23/92	LOS COYOTES/SAVANNA	36	41	5	
4/24/92	CATALINA/AVALON	32	42	10	
4/28/92	IMPERIAL/BREA	37	48	11	
4/29/92	CRESTE VERDE/CORONA	35	37	2	
4/30/92	DM/MAGNOLIA	35	38	3	
5/4/92	LEAGUE FINALS	36	44	8	
	SKYLINKS	20	29	9	
5/11/92	CIF REGIONALS	36	41	5	
	EL DORADO	36	43	7	
TOTAL		1233	1519	286	
AVERAGE		35.2	43.4	8.2	

PUTTS	3 PUTTS	BIRDIES	PARS	BOGIES	DB+	GREENS
13	0	0	2	6	1	0
15	0	0	3	5	1	0
17	1	0	2	0	7	2
17	1	0	1	5	3	1
17	3	0	2	2	5	0
17	2	1	4	2	2	3
15	1	0	1	7	1	0
16	1	0	1	4	4	1
16	2	0	3	3	3	1
14	0	0	3	5	1	1
15	1	0	3	5	1	1
18	1	0	2	3	4	2
13	2	0	4	4	1	2
18	2	2	3	1	3	5
16	2	2	1	3	3	2
19	1	0	3	2	4	3
18	2	0	4	4	1	4
14		0	4	3	2	
16	0	0	2	5	2	2
16	1	1	5	2	1	5
13	0	1	7	1	0	4
18	2	0	2	2	5	1
11	0	0	6	1	2	1
			2	4	3	
16	0	0	3	3	3	2
16	0	1	5	3	0	6
16	1	1	5	2	1	4
		0	2	6	1	
		0	0	1	4	
410	26	9	85	94	69	53
15.8	1.0	0.3	2.9	3.2	2.4	2.1

CAMERON LEE–1997		PAR	SCORE	OVER PAR	
DATE	GOLF COURSE/OPPONENT	PAR	SCORE	PAR	
3/3/97	MILESQUARE/LOS AMIGOS	36	41	5	
3/4/97	DM/GAHR	35	46	11	
3/5/97	LA MIRADA/GAHR	35	43	8	
3/9/97	NAVY BASE/PACIFIC	32	34	2	
3/11/97	DM/EDISON	35	41	6	
3/12/97	CYPRESS CLUB/FOOTHILL	35	44	9	
3/13/97	SEACLIFF CC/EDISON	36	49	13	
3/18/97	DM/LA QUINTA	35	41	6	
3/19/97	PRACTICE @ DM	35	40	5	
3/20/97	DM/LB POLY	35	43	8	
4/1/97	DM/CYPRESS	35	43	8	
4/2/97	DM/VALENCIA	35	40	5	
4/3/97	CYPRESS CLUB/CYPRESS	35	45	10	
4/7/97	MILESQUARE/LA QUINTA	36	43	7	
4/8/99	DM/SAVANNA	35	41	6	
4/10/97	IMPERIAL/BREA	36	44	8	
4/14/97	RECREATION PARK/LB POLY	36	47	11	
4/15/97	DM/MAGNOLIA	35	42	7	
4/17/97	DM/LOARA	35	42	7	
4/21/97	DM/PACIFICA	35	40	5	
4/22/97	ALTA VISTA/VALENCIA	37	45	8	
4/23/97	DM/DOWNEY	35	41	6	
4/24/97	DM/SAVANNA	35	41	6	
4/26/97	CATALINA/AVALON	32	34	2	
4/28/97	RIO HONDO/DOWNEY	36	46	10	
4/29/97	DM/BREA	35	39	4	
5/1/97	DM/MAGNOLIA	35	38	3	
5/5/97	LEAGUE FINALS/DM	35	41	6	
		36	40	4	
5/6/97	LEAGUE FINALS	37	46	9	
	ALTA VISTA	35	40	5	
TOTAL		1090	1300	210	
AVERAGE		35.2	41.9	6.8	

THE CAMERON LEE STORY—
MORE PARS THAN BOGEYS

Cameron Lee came along in 1995, the post-Tiger era. As a result of the Tiger years, there was more interest in golf and the bar for quality was raised at Western High. Cameron was a good golfer going into the 1997 season. His scores averaged 42.2 in his junior year. But in his senior year, 1998, he had his sights set on becoming our

| | 3 | | | | | |
PUTTS	PUTTS	BIRDIES	PARS	BOGIES	DB+	GREENS
12	0	1	2	6	0	0
18	1	0	4	2	3	4
17	1	0	3	4	2	2
12	0	1	5	3	0	2
16	0	1	3	3	2	3
18	1	0	3	3	3	3
18	0	0	2	2	5	2
18	0	0	5	1	2	5
16	1	0	5	3	1	4
16	0	0	3	5	1	1
16	1	1	2	3	4	1
18	1	0	5	3	1	6
16	1	0	2	4	3	1
16	0	0	2	7	0	1
15	0	0	3	6	0	2
18	2	0	2	4	3	2
18	2	0	1	6	2	2
18	0	0	2	7	0	2
18	0	0	2	7	0	2
17	2	1	4	2	2	3
18	1	1	2	3	3	3
18	1	0	4	4	1	3
16	1	0	3	6	0	2
14	0	2	3	4	0	3
15	1	0	2	4	3	0
17	1	0	6	2	1	5
15	1	1	4	4	0	3
18	1	0	4	2	3	6
17	0	0	5	4	0	4
19	2	0	2	5	2	1
13	1	0	4	5	0	1
511	23	9	99	124	47	79
16.5	0.7	0.3	3.2	4.0	1.5	2.5

number-one player. The past year, he had scored in the low 40s consistently, but only had three rounds in the 30s the whole season. He had to be in that range more often to lead the team into competition. Cameron and I mapped out a way for him to achieve his goal for the coming season. For Cameron to move to the next level, we determined he'd have to focus on three areas. First, he'd have to score more pars than bogeys. That meant he'd have to hit more greens in

CAMERON LEE–1998		PAR	SCORE	OVER PAR	
DATE	GOLF COURSE/OPPONENT	PAR	SCORE	PAR	
3/3/98	LA MIRADA/GAHR	35	37	2	
3/4/98	DM/GAHR	35	36	1	
3/5/98	NAVY GC/PACIFICA	32	37	5	
3/9/98	MILESQUARE/LA QUINTA	36	42	6	
3/10/98	LOS COYOTES/ LA QUINTA	36	50	13	
3/11/98	DM/LOS AMIGOS	35	37	2	
3/12/98	MILESQUARE/LOS AMIGOS	36	40	4	
3/16/98	SKYLINKS/JORDAN	36	36	0	
3/17/98	LOS COYOTES/JORDAN	36	37	1	
3/18/98	MESA LINDA/COSTA MESA	35	44	9	
3/19/98	EMPIRE LAKES/ALTA LOMA	36	41	5	
3/23/98	RANCHO PARK/LACES	35	40	5	
3/24/98	ALTA VISTA/VALENCIA	37	41	4	
3/26/98	DM/SAVANNA	33	37	4	
3/30/98	CYPRESS/AVALON	36	45	9	
3/31/98	DM/BREA	35	41	6	
4/2/98	LOS COYOTES/MAGNOLIA	36	41	5	
4/6/98	LA PURISMA	36	40	4	
		36	55	19	
4/7/98	MARSCHALLIA RANCH	35	40	5	
		37	41	4	
4/8/98	ALISAL-RIVER	36	38	2	
		36	40	4	
4/13/98	DM/ALUMNI	35	42	7	
4/15/98	LC/CENTENNIAL	36	43	7	
4/16/98	DM/VALENCIA	35	40	5	
4/20/98	DM/LACES	35	39	4	
4/21/98	LC/SAVANNA	36	41	5	
4/23/98	WEST HILLS/BREA	35	42	7	
4/28/98	DM/MAGNOLIA	35	37	2	
4/29/98	PK/CENTENNIAL	36	39	3	
4/30/98	LC/ALTA LOMA	36	43	7	
5/4/98	DAD MILLER	35	38	3	
		36	45	9	
5/5/98	LOS COYOTES	36	39	3	
		36	39	3	
5/7/98	ALTA VISTA	37	40	3	
		35	40	5	
TOTAL		1320	1543	192	
AVERAGE		34.7	40.6	5.1	

PUTTS	3 PUTTS	BIRDIES	PARS	BOGIES	DB+	GREENS
17	1	1	5	3	0	6
14	0	0	8	1	0	4
15	1	1	4	2	2	2
15	0	0	4	4	1	2
19	2	0	2	3	4	2
18	1	1	6	2	0	5
15	1	1	4	3	1	3
16	0	2	5	2	0	7
13	0	1	6	2	0	3
19	2	0	2	5	2	2
20	2	1	4	3	1	5
19	2	1	2	6	0	5
16	1	0	6	2	1	5
16	2	1	3	5	0	5
19	2	0	3	4	2	2
20	3	0	3	6	0	6
16	0	1	3	4	1	3
17	0	1	4	3	1	5
21	3	0	0	2	7	0
20	3	1	3	4	1	6
14	0	0	5	4	0	2
15	1	0	7	2	0	4
17	0	1	3	5	0	4
20	3	1	3	3	2	4
15	0	0	2	7	0	1
17	1	0	6	2	1	4
18	2	1	4	3	1	6
19	3	0	4	5	0	5
16	1	0	5	2	2	2
17	1	0	7	2	0	5
17	1	0	6	3	0	3
17	2	1	2	5	1	0
15	0	0	6	3	0	4
17	0	0	3	4	2	1
16	0	2	2	5	0	4
17	2	1	4	4	0	6
17	1	1	4	4	0	5
16	0	2	3	2	2	5
645	44	23	153	131	35	143
17.0	1.2	0.6	4.0	3.4	0.9	3.8

regulation. In 1997, he'd only hit 2.5 greens per nine in regulation. Second, he'd have to practice his putting so that once he hit the greens, he'd get down in two or less. Those two areas led to the third, increasing his birdies. He'd accomplish that when he could combine those first two, hitting greens and putting well. The more he could succeed in all three areas, the more times he'd score in the 30s.

How would he get there? The answer, not surprisingly, was more range time. Our plan called for range practice twice a week from June through February, plus lots of time on the putting green. The only way Cameron was going to achieve his goals was by practicing, not playing. Unfortunately, since he came along after Tiger, he had only heard of Tiger's practice regimens but hadn't had them rub off directly. I was forced to preach instead of just pointing to an inspiration on the practice tee.

Then, as we were putting our plan together, we got lucky. I got a call from Terry Titus, the head pro at a local course called Cypress. He said they needed a cart assistant, and if I had anyone to send him down for an interview. I sent Cameron over, and he got the job. Unlike at the navy course where I had placed kids before, at Cypress the employees can only play one day a week. But they can hit balls on the range all they want. It was an ideal, built-in discipline. Even if Cameron was tempted to play instead of practice, he wasn't allowed to. So he practiced and practiced, until he became a practice addict.

Did it pay off? Take a look at his 1998 Master Card stats. He achieved success in two of the goals we had set. He hit more greens in regulation, which almost inevitably led to more pars than bogeys. And he increased his birdies by 156 percent, from nine to twenty-three. As a result, Cameron had fourteen rounds in the 30s, compared to only three in the previous year.

However, Cameron didn't quite achieve everything he was after. His overall average score dropped from 42.2 in 1997 to 40.6 in 1998, a dramatic improvement, but not where he wanted to be. Why? Putting. He didn't practice on the green as much as he intended. In fact, while he was becoming an outstanding player from tee to green, he actually had more three-putt greens in 1998 than in 1997. That was the only thing that kept him from being a consistent 30s golfer.

Cameron's next goal would be perfecting his putting in order to make more birdies than pars. Remember, the higher your handicap, the easier it is to take strokes off your score. The lower your handicap, the more diligence it takes to bring your score down. It's a mixed blessing. You're now good enough to hone the last few strokes of your game. But the last few are the most resistant. Overall, though, it's a good problem to have. It's the one faced by the best of golfers, even those headed for the PGA Tour . . . which, of course, brings us back to Tiger.

Whoever Said Statistics Are Dry Never Read Tiger's

Take a look at Tiger's four Master Cards, from 1991, '92, '93, and '94. You're reading, stat by stat, the story of a prodigy breaking through.

During Tiger's first year at Western, our home course was Dad Miller. It was a fun course for most of the guys, but it quickly got too easy for Tiger. Over the year he was one over par, which was astounding for a freshman but not astounding for a Tiger. Think of it this way. If you're a very good player, you may be one or two over per round, which means after thirty to thirty-five rounds you're maybe thirty-five to fifty over for the year. He was one over for the whole year! He may have been only fourteen years old, but he needed more of a challenge. Tiger could only realize his potential if he could hone his game on a more sophisticated, more daunting golf course.

I took our case to Chuck McCauley, the owner of Los Coyotes Country Club, and I begged and pleaded with him to let us use his course. Fortunately, Chuck had seen Tiger play in the Lee Hamill

| TIGER WOODS–1991 | | | | OVER | |
DATE	GOLF COURSE/OPPONENT	PAR	SCORE	PAR	
2/25/91	DAD MILLER/GAHR	34	34	0.0	
2/26/91	RECREATION PARK/POLY	36	38	2.0	
3/4/91	DAD MILLER/ESPERANZA	34	36	2.0	
3/5/91	YORBA LINDA CC/ESPERANZA	35	38	3.0	
3/6/91	REC PARK/WILSON	36	34	-2.0	
3/7/91	DAD MILLER/EDISON	34	32	-2.0	
3/11/91	DAD MILLER/LAKEWOOD	34	33	-1.0	
3/12/91	SKYLINKS/LAKEWOOD	36	36	0.0	
3/14/91	DAD MILLER/WILSON	34	33	-1.0	
3/18/91	DAD MILLER/COSTA MESA	34	35	1.0	
3/19/91	SEACLIFF CC/EDISON	36	44	8.0	
3/21/91	LA MIRADA/GAHR	35	33	-2.0	
4/1/91	DAD MILLER/ MARINA	34	34	0.0	
4/2/91	DAD MILLER/VALENCIA	34	33	-1.0	
4/3/91	COSTA MESA/COSTA MESA	35	35	0.0	
4/4/91	DAD MILLER/SAVANNA	34	32	-2.0	
4/8/91	MEADOWLARK/MARINA	35	35	0.0	
4/9/91	IMPERIAL/BREA	37	35	-2.0	
4/11/91	DAD MILLER/LB POLY	34	34	0.0	
4/15/91	DAD MILLER/LA QUINTA	34	36	2.0	
4/17/91	FULLERTON/SERVITE	33	37	4.0	
4/18/91	ALTA VISTA/VALENCIA	37	37	0.0	
4/22/91	MILESQUARE/LA QUINTA	36	33	-3.0	
4/23/91	DAD MILLER/SAVANNA	34	31	-3.0	
4/24/91	DAD MILLER/MAGNOLIA	34	34	0.0	
4/25/91	DM/BREA	34	34	0.0	
4/26/91	CATALINA/SERVITE	32	34	2.0	
4/29/91	SKYLINKS	36	35	-1.0	
		36	33	-3.0	
4/30/91	LB RECREATION PARK	36	37	1.0	
		36	36	0.0	
5/2/91	EL DORADO	36	38	2.0	
		34	36	2.0	
5/6/91	MESA VERDE	36	34	-2.0	
		35	36	1.0	
5/20/91	CANYON CC/PALM SPRINGS	35	36	1.0	
		37	32	-5.0	
6/3/91	MARBELLA CC	35	36	1.0	
	AM ROUND	35	35	0.0	
	PM ROUND	35	35	0.0	
		35	32	-3.0	
TOTAL		1432	1431	-1.0	
AVERAGE		34.9	34.9	0.0	

PUTTS	3 PUTTS	BIRDIES	PARS	BOGIES	DB+	GREENS
16	0	1	7	1	0	7
17	1	1	6	1	1	5
18	0	0	7	2	0	7
17	1	1	5	2	1	3
14	1	2	7	0	0	3
15	0	2	6	1	0	6
13	0	1	7	1	0	6
16	1	1	7	1	0	6
16	1	3	4	2	0	7
17	3	2	4	3	0	2
17	0	1	4	3	1	5
12	0	3	5	1	0	6
16	1	2	5	2	0	6
14	0	3	4	2	0	6
15	0	2	6	0	1	6
16	1	4	3	2	0	7
16	0	0	9	0	0	7
16	0	2	7	0	0	9
17	2	3	3	3	0	8
19	2	1	5	3	0	8
18	2	1	3	5	0	5
16	1	1	7	1	0	7
12	0	3	6	0	0	8
15	1	3	6	0	0	8
16	0	2	5	2	0	7
15	1	2	5	2	0	5
13	0	0	7	2	0	3
		2	6	1	0	
		4	4	1	0	
		2	4	3	0	
		2	5	2	0	
		1	5	3	0	
		0	7	2	0	
		3	5	1	0	
		2	4	3	0	
		0	8	1	0	
		4	5	0	0	
13	0	2	5	1	1	4
16	1	1	7	1	0	7
15	0	1	7	1	0	6
13	0	4	4	1	0	7
479	20	75	226	63	5	187
15.5	0.6	1.8	5.5	1.5	0.1	6.0

| TIGER WOODS–1992 | | | | OVER | |
DATE	GOLF COURSE/OPPONENT	PAR	SCORE	PAR	
3/4/92	LA MIRADA/GAHR	35	37	2.0	
3/9/92	RECREATION PARK/LB POLY	36	33	-3.0	
3/10/92	MESA VERDE/ESTANCIA	36	36	0.0	
3/11/92	LOS COYOTES/LB POLY	36	39	3.0	
3/12/92	SEACLIFF CC/ EDISON	36	35	-1.0	
3/16/92	DAD MILLER/EDISON	35	33	-2.0	
3/17/92	YORBA LINDA CC/ESPERANZA	35	36	1.0	
3/18/92	LOS COYOTES/ESPERANZA	36	40	4.0	
3/19/92	LOS COTOTES/LA QUINTA	36	37	1.0	
3/23/92	MILESQUARE/LA QUINTA	36	35	-1.0	
3/24/92	LOS COYOTES/WILSON	36	37	1.0	
3/26/92	ALTA VISTA CC/VALENCIA	37	36	-1.0	
3/30/92	RECREATION PARK/WILSON	36	37	1.0	
3/31/92	DAD MILLER/SAVANNA	35	34	-1.0	
4/2/92	LOS COYOTES/BREA	36	37	1.0	
4/6/92	MEADOWLARK/MARINA	35	36	1.0	
4/8/92	LOS COY/GAHR & ESTANCIA	36	34	-2.0	
4/10/92	SKYLINKS/AVALON	36	40	4.0	
4/13/92	RANCHO CANADA-E/WSI	35	34	-1.0	
		36	35	-1.0	
4/14/92	RANCHO CANADA-W/WSI	36	37	1.0	
		35	37	2.0	
4/20/92	DAD MILLER/MARINA	35	32	-3.0	
4/21/92	ALTA VISTA/CORONA	37	37	0.0	
4/22/92	LOS COYOTES/VALENCIA	36	41	5.0	
4/23/92	LOS COYOTES/SAVANNA	36	35	-1.0	
4/24/92	CATALINA IS/AVALON	32	37	5.0	
4/28/92	IMPERIAL/BREA	37	37	0.0	
4/29/92	CRESTE VERDE/CORONA	35	34	-1.0	
4/30/92	DAD MILLER/MAGNOLIA	35	31	-4.0	
5/4/92	SKYLINKS	36	32	-4.0	
		20	21	1.0	
5/5/92	RECREATION PARK	36	38	2.0	
		36	34	-2.0	
5/7/92	EL DORADO	36	36	0.0	
		36	35	-1.0	
5/11/92	REGIONALS/EL DORADO	36	35	-1.0	
		36	35	-1.0	
5/26/92	HACIENDA CC	35	36	1.0	
		36	40	4.0	
TOTAL		1412	1421	9.0	
AVERAGE		35.3	35.5	0.2	

PUTTS	3 PUTTS	BIRDIES	PARS	BOGIES	DB+	GREENS
15	0	1	5	3	0	6
12	0	4	4	1	0	6
17	1	2	5	2	0	6
17	1	1	5	2	1	5
14	0	1	8	0	0	6
14	1	2	7	0	0	6
14	1	1	6	2	0	5
14	0	1	5	1	2	5
16	2	2	4	3	0	6
14	0	4	3	1	1	6
17	1	2	5	1	1	6
15	0	3	4	2	0	6
15	0	1	6	2	0	5
16	0	2	5	1	0	8
17	0	0	8	1	0	7
18	2	2	5	1	1	8
16	0	2	7	0	0	9
17	2	2	2	4	1	4
15	0	4	4	1	0	8
16	0	1	7	1	0	7
14	0	1	8	0	0	7
		1	4	2	2	
15	0	2	5	1	1	6
17	0	2	6	1	0	8
16	2	5	2	2	0	9
		4	5	0	0	
		0	4	1	0	
		1	5	3	0	
		3	5	1	0	
		0	9	0	0	
		3	5	0	1	
		2	6	1	0	
		2	6	1	0	
		1	6	2	0	
		0	6	2	1	
371	13	65	187	46	12	155
15.5	0.5	1.9	5.3	1.3	0.3	6.5

TIGER WOODS–1994				OVER	
DATE	GOLF COURSE/OPPONENT	PAR	SCORE	PAR	
2/28/94	DAD MILLER/ALUMNI	35	35	0	
3/1/94	COSTA MESA/COSTA MESA	35	36	1	
3/2/94	LOS COYOTES/COSTA MESA	36	34	-2	
3/3/94	LOS COYOTES/AVALON	36	36	0	
3/7/94	RECREATION PARK/LB POLY	36	35	-1	
3/8/94	WESTERN HILLS/EL DORADO	35	37	2	
3/10/94	LOS COYOTES/LB POLY	36	37	1	
3/22/94	DAD MILLER/SAVANNA	35	33	-2	
3/23/94	RANCHO SAN JOAQ./IRVINE	36	34	-2	
3/24/94	LOS COYOTES/BREA	36	37	1	
3/28/94	BRITISH COLUMBIA TOUR	36	35	-1	
	OLYMPIC VIEW	36	38	2	
3/29/94	BCT TOUR	36	36	0	
	OLYMPIC VIEW	36	34	-2	
4/4/94	DAD MILLER/LOARA	35	33	-2	
4/5/94	LOS COYOTES/MAGNOLIA	36	36	0	
4/7/94	LOS COYOTES/ALUMNI	36	39	3	
4/11/94	CYPRESS CLUB/EL TORO	35	36	1	
4/12/94	ALTA VISTA/VALENCIA	37	35	-2	
4/13/94	LOS COYOTES/IRVINE	36	35	-1	
4/14/94	DAD MILLER/SAVANNA	35	30	-5	
4/19/94	IMPERIAL/BREA	36	34	-2	
4/20/94	LOS COYOTES/LOARA	36	34	-2	
4/21/94	DAD MILLER/MAGNOLIA	35	32	-3	
4/22/94	CATALINA IS./AVALON	32	30	-2	
4/26/94	LOS COYOTES/CENTENNIAL	36	35	-1	
4/27/94	ET MARINE BASE/EL TORO	36	36	0	
4/28/94	LOS COYOTES/VALENCIA	36	33	-3	
5/3/94	DAD MILLER	35	33	-2	
		36	35	-1	
5/4/94	LOS COYOTES	36	34	-2	
		36	34	-2	
5/6/94	ALTA VISTA	37	33	-4	
		35	35	0	
5/10/94	GREEN RIVER-ORANGE	36	35	-1	
		35	35	0	
5/23/94	LA CUMBRE	35	30	-5	
	SANTA BARBARA	36	36	0	
TOTAL		1354	1315	-39	
AVERAGE		35.6	34.6	-1.0	

PUTTS	3 PUTTS	BIRDIES	PARS	BOGIES	DB+	GREENS
15	0	2	5	2	0	5
16	0	2	4	3	0	6
13	0	3	5	1	0	6
17	0	0	9	0	0	8
14	0	2	6	1	0	5
17	1	1	5	3	0	6
17	0	1	7	0	1	8
15	0	3	4	2	0	7
15	0	3	5	1	0	8
13	0	0	8	1	0	3
15	1	2	5	2	0	5
18	1	2	5	0	2	5
16	0	1	7	1	0	7
11	0	4	3	1	1	5
15	0	3	5	1	0	5
16	1	1	7	1	0	7
15	1	0	6	3	0	3
17	0	2	5	2	0	5
16	0	2	6	1	0	7
12	0	3	4	2	0	4
14	0	5	4	0	0	8
17	1	3	5	1	0	9
16	0	2	7	0	0	9
16	2	4	3	2	0	8
17	0	3	5	1	0	8
13	0	3	4	2	0	5
17	2	2	4	3	0	8
14	0	4	4	1	0	8
14	0	3	5	1	0	6
12	0	1	8	0	0	4
15	1	3	5	1	0	8
18	0	2	7	0	0	9
14	1	4	4	1	0	8
15	0	1	7	1	0	6
		3	3	2	1	
		4	1	4	0	
11	0	5	4	0	0	7
16	0	2	6	0	1	8
542	12	91	197	48	6	234
15.1	0.3	2.4	5.2	1.3	0.2	6.5

Junior Tournament and had a weakness for watching a superstar in the making. He called back after about ten days and said, yes, we could use Los Coyotes as our home course, and no, they weren't even going to charge us!

Look at Tiger's stat sheets from '91 to '92 and you can see how much tougher Los Coyotes is than Dad Miller. Tiger went from one over to nine over for the season. Again, that would be great for most any high school player (and the rest of us), but not for a fifteen-year-old with his eye on a Masters jacket. Tiger concentrated hard on his stats, and when he saw his over-par numbers climbing higher than his birdies, he asked me, "Coach, how many more times are we going to go back and play Dad Miller this year?" We still played there in between playing Los Coyotes. Tiger knew every time we were at Dad Miller he'd be three or four under par and that would bring his overall average down. In any case, it appears that he finished the season worse than his first year, but actually his game was improving greatly.

By the time his junior year came, Tiger was playing in a lot of professional tournaments (the L.A. Open, Ben Hogan and Byron Nelson events, and a few others) and sometimes he had to miss some of our matches. But the combination of outside play and tougher courses on our schedule just kept improving his game. By the time we finished our season, Tiger had won his second California Interscholastic Federation Title at Canyon Country Club. He shot a four-under-par 68! At the age of sixteen! And for the year, even playing on much more difficult courses, he was five under par.

That put him, cumulatively for his first three years, three over par. He knew where he stood, and he wanted to finish under par for his entire high school career. That meant he would have to play at least as well in his senior year as he had in his junior year.

Did he do it? Did he ever! He literally took his game to another level. He was basically the same player for those first three years at Western High, just maturing, learning more about courses and clubs. But look at his Master Card for his senior year. You can track

Tiger's breakthrough from April 12 on. Starting then, he had seven straight rounds under par. They were written up in the local papers and picked up by wire services and some papers outside the area. He was under par for thirteen out of fourteen rounds. He ended the year thirty-nine under par! Remember, this was on the tougher courses we now played.

Take a close look at some of the specifics within his stats. He had ninety-one birdies and eagles. Talk about more birdies than pars! He had only forty-eight bogies for the whole season. He was either on the par 5s in two or right on the fringe so he could turn them into eagles.

How about Tiger's goal of finishing his high school career under par? He was three over for the first three years, but with his thirty-nine-under senior year he closed out his high school career thirty-four shots under par. And Tiger Woods wasn't quite eighteen years old.

Not surprisingly, the first semester of Tiger's senior year was one long speculation about where he was going to college. He'd been recruited by just about every place that had a golf team and a golf course, or might be willing to build one if he'd come there. And, on top of his golf prowess, Tiger had the grades to go anywhere. The question of the year was, where? Recruiters were sniffing around, reporters were calling, and other kids at Western all wanted to know. But Tiger kept it secret until the last minute.

Finally, in November, he got down to University of Nevada–Las Vegas and Stanford, each of which had compelling attractions for Tiger. We held a press conference, a first for Western High, with television and newspapers reporters, plus writers from *Sports Illustrated,* ESPN, and *Golf Digest.* Tiger had hats from both of the schools sitting on the table in front of him. When it came time to make his announcement, Tiger shuffled the hats around, put the UNLV hat under the table, and put the Stanford hat in front of him. But he didn't put it on. At the time, our school had a rule that students couldn't wear any hat except one from Western, because of the meanings hats could carry as far as gang affiliations. One of the reporters, who obviously didn't know anything about gangs and colors and such, asked Tiger if he wasn't going to put the Stanford hat on. Tiger said, no, he couldn't because it wasn't a Western hat. But some of the media people asked the principal if it would be okay for Tiger to wear the hat just for this one day so they could take pictures. Even the principal gave in for the day.

In January of Tiger's senior year, he was honored as the 1993 Dial High School Athlete Scholar of the United States. In order to win, we had to send the Dial Corporation all sorts of stats and results, plus his GPA and other distinctions like belonging to the National Honor Society. The Dial Award put Tiger in the company of previous winners like Herschel Walker, Todd Marinovich, Kevin Wilhite, Chris Spielman, Derrick Brooks, and, the year before, Amanda White and Jacque Vaughn.

For the presentation, Tiger, his mom and dad, and my wife and I all went to Washington, D.C., to a banquet at the Washington Hilton that was part of the Washington Redskins Touchdown Club awards. There was a head table that went on forever, with at least eighty people. Tiger was sitting up there surrounded by stars. Right next to him was Kristin Folkl, the volleyball star and female Dial winner, who also ended up going to Stanford.

Tiger's stat sheets don't have any columns for getting recruited by colleges, choosing Stanford, dodging *Sports Illustrated* reporters, or winning the Dial Award. But every number there contributed to the outcome, the best year any high school golfer has ever had.

YOUR STORY

At the beginning of this book, I said our goal was to take up to ten shots off your score and do it simply and practically, while having some fun along the way. It's nice to whack the ball and it's pleasant to go for a walk in the sunshine. But golf is about scoring. It's a competition, not only between you and your opponents but between you and the golf course. So naturally, you want to lower your score. But you don't want to spend the rest of your life, or life savings, in that pursuit.

I think I've offered you some simple ways to cut strokes off your game. It's not enough just to want to lower your handicap from a fourteen to a nine or your scores from low 90s to mid 80s. You don't have to change everything about your game, and you don't have to turn it from pleasure into work, but you need to practice the parts you can change and you need to keep a record of your results. You sure want to know if you're making progress. That's why you carry a scorecard, and that's why you should keep track of not only your score but your tee shots, green hits, putts, pars, bogeys, and birdies.

I've included some sample stat sheets. I suggest you either create your own on a computer or make copies of these. Fill them in. Find the areas of your game that need to be addressed. Get out there and practice those specifics. Plot your progress. Improvement feels good. It leads to more improvement. Think of yourself as if you were one of my high school players. If they can get good enough to win a league championship in just a few weeks, you can improve your game in a few weeks too. You may not turn into Tiger Woods, but you can use the same lessons he learned, the same techniques he employed. If you do what he does and it only works half as well for you, that's pretty good. Right?

One more thing. After you read this book, I hope you practice and play a lot. And I hope that sometimes you take a break and don't play.

What's that about? You just told me to practice all the time, didn't you? More, yes. All the time, no. Just like I told my daughter, who played club soccer and softball for several years, if she didn't feel good about going to another game right after the previous one, she should speak up. I told her, "I'll tell the coach you're not feeling well." It would be the truth. When you overdo something, even something you love, you don't feel good about it. Some pressure is good for character. Too much pressure backfires.

Tiger's father, Earl, and I had the same discussion when Tiger started at Western. We knew Tiger would be not only playing in our league matches but competing in major championships as well. Besides that, Tiger was a driven student. And, don't forget, he was only a teenager. I gave him a free, no-guilt pass in advance. "When the pressure heats up and gets too hot, take a day to cool off." In four years, he took me up on it only a few times. To his credit, I don't recall him ever taking a day off when we absolutely had to have him to win.

The lesson is, stop once in a while. Practice two or three days a week, not four or five. Play twice or three times a week, or, when you're on vacation a little more, but not every day. Take a day to remember how you played, to think about how you'll play next time, but mostly to think about other things—your job, your family, your hobbies. Don't become a workaholic about work or play. Believe it or not, people who take breaks perform better than ones who never let up.

Now, go out and enjoy the game. Practice that improves your game is fun. Better tee shots, fairway irons, sand shots, and putts are fun. Lower your score. Lower your handicap. Beat your friends. That's even more fun.

INSIGHT: Not knowing your statistics is a handicap.

LESSON: How to Keep Your Stats

- **The Crosby Card**—use whole score square on card.
  - center: total strokes on hole
  - upper left: in fairway (or not)
  - upper right: dot to indicate on green in regulation
  - lower left: in trap (or not)
  - lower right: number of putts

- **The Master Card**—scorecard of scorecards.
  - Spreadsheet of key data across top:
    date, course, par, score per nine or eighteen,
    over/under par, putts per round, three-putts +,
    birdies, pars, bogeys, double-bogeys +, greens
    in regulation
  - At bottom
    totals and averages

Identify what needs work. Work on it.

Lower your score. Beat your friends. Have fun.

NAME				OVER/	
DATE	GOLF COURSE	PAR	SCORE	UNDER PAR	
TOTAL					
AVERAGE					

	PUTTS	3 PUTTS	BIRDIES	PARS	BOGIES	DB+	GREENS

DATE	GOLF COURSE	PAR	SCORE	OVER/ UNDER PAR	
NAME					
TOTAL					
AVERAGE					

	PUTTS	3 PUTTS	BIRDIES	PARS	BOGIES	DB+	GREENS

NAME				OVER/	
DATE	GOLF COURSE	PAR	SCORE	UNDER PAR	
TOTAL					
AVERAGE					

	PUTTS	3 PUTTS	BIRDIES	PARS	BOGIES	DB+	GREENS

NAME				OVER/	
DATE	GOLF COURSE	PAR	SCORE	UNDER PAR	
TOTAL					
AVERAGE					

	PUTTS	3 PUTTS	BIRDIES	PARS	BOGIES	DB+	GREENS

NAME				OVER/	
DATE	GOLF COURSE	PAR	SCORE	UNDER PAR	
TOTAL					
AVERAGE					

	PUTTS	3 PUTTS	BIRDIES	PARS	BOGIES	DB+	GREENS

NAME				OVER/	
DATE	GOLF COURSE	PAR	SCORE	UNDER PAR	
TOTAL					
AVERAGE					

		3					
	PUTTS	PUTTS	BIRDIES	PARS	BOGIES	DB+	GREENS